Help, Lord! I'm Having a Senior Moment—Again!

A WINGSHOOTER'S GUIDE TO MONTANA

If you would like to order additional copies of this book, or any other Wilderness Adventures Press, Inc. publication, please fill out the order form below or call **1-800-925-3339** or **fax: 406-763-4911**.

Mail to:
Wilderness Adventures Press, P.O. Box 1410, Bozeman, MT 59771.

Ship to:

Name: _____

Address: _____

City: _____ State: _____ Zip Code: _____

Home Phone: _____ Work Phone: _____

Payment: ☐Check ☐Visa ☐Mastercard ☐Discover

Card Number: _____ Exp. Date: _____

Signature: _____

Quantity	Title of Book & Author	Price	Total
	Total Order + shipping & handling		

Please add $3.00 per book for shipping and handling.

Coming in 1996 from Wilderness Adventures Press

Wingshooter's Guide to South Dakota AND *Wingshooter's Guide to Arizona*

Reserve Your Copy Now!

Dedication

For my husband, Charles Flowers, forever my
favorite "senior."

*Even to your old age and gray hairs I am he, I am he who will
sustain you. I have made you and I will carry you;
I will sustain you and I will rescue you.*

ISAIAH 46:4

Contents

*P*art 1:
Laugh-Out-Loud Moments

Part 2:
Surprising Moments

Part 3:
Embarrassing Moments

$\mathcal{P}$art 4:
Grateful Moments

$\mathscr{P}$art 5:
Tug-at-the-Heart Moments

Acknowledgments

The author wishes to thank the following men and women for contributing their ideas and experiences—all of which have been woven into the fabric of this book.

Barbara Anson · Warren Babcock · Carole Barnes · Mary Battmer · Maureen Bavoillot · Bee Beeman · Linda Bowman · Hal Britton · Cori Brown · Lenore Byrnes · Norma Casey · Joan Clayton · Dolores Collins · Jeanne Dixon · Regina Engler · Marilou Flinkman · Charles Flowers · Sharon Foster · Darrell Gilliam · Viola Gommer · Vicki Granros · Elinor Bridy Grossman · Judy Hampton · Shelley Hussey · Rose Jackson · Anita Janvier · Edwin Jaqua · Susan Jones · Violette Koons · Carole Lewis · Pat Lewis · Liz Livingston · Deanna Luke · Nell Main · Ramona McKenzie · Lynda McNeal · Susan Titus Osborn · Ellie Owen · Laurel Phillips · Marie Pinschmidt · Mary Ella Ray · Karen Robertson · Martha Rogers · Arline Signorella · Karen Stringfield · Anne Subia · Terri Sutor · Paul Sutton · Karen Swanson · Diana Taylor · Pat Van Gorder · June Varnum · Susan Wallace · Claudia Ward · Jeanne Zornes

Introduction

In my first book about senior moments, I quoted my mother-in-law, Ada Flowers, who once said, "Growing old is not for sissies!" I mentioned that it took my husband and me another 20 years to "get it." We had to reach that sixth decade first!

Here I am with a second book on the subject of those pesky senior moments, deeper still into my 60s, and even more aware of the truth of Ada's statement.

I'm also laughing more and struggling with life less, for I'm realizing that wisdom comes with age, and therefore life after 50, 60, 70 and more is truly worthwhile and deeply satisfying. I'm no sissy! And I hope you will say the same thing about yourself as you read this book and enjoy the funny antics we put ourselves through as we age. I hope you'll also relate to the poignant moments that are also very much a part of being a "senior."

I pray these new notes to God in the following pages (some of my own, and some based on the funny and touching contributions I've received from other seniors—both men and women) will encourage you, bring a smile and perhaps a tear, and even a sigh of recognition as you relate to everyone who has joined the over-the-hill gang.

As you read, I encourage you to lean on the Lord for strength, understanding, wisdom and peace in everything you think, say and do. He said He "will never leave you nor forsake you" (Deut. 31:6). You can count on that, and when you do, you will age with grace and gratitude—counting all of life good.

Part I:
Laugh-Out-Loud
Moments

Angel Food

Dear God:

I was sorry to hear about Carl's death. I know it's going to be hard for Marion. They were married for 45 years. And she was so devoted to keeping Carl healthy so he'd be around for a long time. Sometimes it was a real drag to be with them. Marion was a broken record (make that CD) on the subject of healthy eating. She prepared lots of veggies, bran muffins from scratch, raw fruit at every meal and plenty of fresh, purified water. Carl went along with the plan because he loved her, but I could see the mischief in his eyes when she wasn't looking.

Their friend Henry told me that when he and Carl met for lunch and Marion wasn't around, Carl indulged himself—chocolate cake (sometimes two big slices), hot fudge sundaes, eggs cooked in bacon grease. He loved them all.

He used to joke about what it would be like in heaven! He could just imagine St. Peter ushering him through the pearly gates and for miles all around there'd be a huge buffet table filled with all the goodies he wanted. "And imagine," he said chuckling, "there's no disease and no pain in heaven, so I won't have to watch what I eat. No cholesterol to check either!"

Henry said he could picture his dear friend looking down on him and shouting, "Henry, it's great up here. No diets, no exercise regimes, no restrictions, no bran muffins. If I'd have known all this ahead of time, I'd have come a lot sooner."

Heaven does sound heavenly at this point in my life. There are still so many things to deal with on this side of eternity. Sometimes I ache for the time when I won't forget where I laid my glasses, if I brushed my teeth or not and what my own phone number is. But then I stop and realize it's wrong to wish my life away. You'll bring me "home" soon enough. Meanwhile, pass the bran muffins.

LORD, I HAVE TO CHUCKLE WHEN I THINK of how much I exaggerate things. I make a big deal out of health issues, politics, religious beliefs and family relationships. They are all temporary. Help me to relax and "be still" (Ps. 46:10), knowing that You are God and You are in charge.

Passport Retort

Dear God:

Dick was thrilled to be invited to speak at the conference in the Philippines. Thank You, Lord, for giving my husband such a gift at this stage of his life. But that meant locating his passport to see if it was still current. He looked in the usual places at home, then in his office at work. All he found was one that had expired 15 years ago.

He called the passport office to apply for a new one. The clerk said that according to the record, Dick had renewed his in 2000. Dick vigorously denied ever having done so. Then he was further upset by the requirement that he file a missing passport report. Add to that a replacement fee of $230, an expense neither of us had expected or planned for, and frustration mounted faster than steam over a boiling kettle.

I threw up a quick prayer of defense, since I was his target! Then suddenly it hit me. Maybe Dick's passport was with mine since we usually travel together. To our relief it was right there in the drawer where I had envisioned it. Thank You, God!

At that moment it all came back. Dick remembered that we had renewed our passports for our fiftieth-anniversary Alaskan cruise in 2000, a fact that he had totally forgotten up until then.

And no, he did not get back the $230! That was one expensive senior moment.

BUT FOR YOU, O GOD, I'd still be upset about the whole thing—the money, the frustration, the forgetfulness. But You are a healing balm to my spirit. You provide everything I need, including a listening ear when I simply need to vent!

$\mathscr{P}$hoto Op

Dear God:

I was thrilled when the president of our homeowners' association invited me to dress up like a bunny and hand out Easter candy to the kids at the clubhouse. The party chairman had hired a photographer so the boys and girls could have their picture taken with the Easter Bunny. I decided to order a few prints myself and share them with friends and family.

Several neighbors volunteered to decorate tables and walls, and my husband offered to help me pick out just the right costume. I knew we'd all have a wonderful afternoon. On the day of the event I was stoked!

I made sure I looked especially nice. I had my hair done that morning, applied makeup carefully and added an extra dollop of mascara for the photo op. The first photo went well. I smiled my best. After about 10 shots, though, I was growing weary of smiling. It was beginning to feel like a burden, yet I didn't want to disappoint any of the families, so I carried on.

After an hour of smiling for the camera and handing out candy, I was ready to call it quits. My feet hurt and my cheeks ached. After the last child received her treat, I went behind the scene and stepped out of the costume. As I pulled off the headpiece and hung it up, I burst out laughing. I had spent an entire afternoon smiling from ear to ear—for no reason. The bunny head covered my face completely. No one could see my face—only the bunny's. His slapstick smile was the only one captured on film.

HOW FUNNY IS THAT, GOD? I didn't even "get" it till it was too late. Does that remind You of something? It reminds me of the way I am with You a lot of the time—a bit clueless! But I know You love me anyway and You're helping me make changes where I need to. That's the good news I cling to each and every day. I want to smile for You—regardless of the situation.

$\mathscr{S}$houlder Pads

Dear God:

It seems You're going to have to assign a special agent/angel to follow me around 24/7. I've got to get a grip. Today, my wife, Lisa, bought me a three-pack of athletic socks. They were on sale for $3.99. Can't pass up such a great deal.

The problem is we no sooner got home than I lost them, or maybe I should say "misplaced" them. That does sound better, doesn't it? It gives me hope that I'm not a "loser."

Anyway, I had a tennis match lined up for 1:00 P.M., and I was looking forward to sporting my new socks to go along with the new sneakers I had purchased the week before.

I was sure I had laid them on the kitchen table, cut off the tags and then placed them on top of my tennis shoes, so they'd be handy when I was ready to get dressed. Wrong again. I couldn't find them anywhere, and I mean anywhere. I looked in every room and even searched my dresser and closet. They were nowhere in sight.

"Lisa," I called from the hallway in despair. "What is going on with me? We just brought the new socks home and I've up and lost them already."

Lisa joined me in the search—but then stopped short and burst out laughing. "Have you tried your shoulders?" she asked, stifling a critical remark, I could tell.

"My shoulders? What are you talking about?" I asked annoyed.

Sure enough, there they were. It all came back to me. After I unwrapped the package and cut off the tags, I slung them over my shoulder and walked around for the next half hour, wondering what I had done.

Send help, pronto, dear Lord. I'm desperate!

GOD, I'M GLAD YOU DON'T give up on me when I give up on myself. You never think of me as a loser. You remind me daily that I am a winner because of what Jesus did for me.

Muscle Men

Dear God:

I overheard my husband talking to my dad this week. For two men, one 58 years old and the other 88, they certainly have a lot in common. Dad told Frank he was having a hard time walking—that his legs and feet seemed to be "on strike."

"I know what you mean," Frank replied. "When I stand up I wait awhile before I walk—to make sure my muscles know what I'm planning to do."

I laughed when I heard about this later in the day. I could picture the two of them standing, taking a moment and then having a word or two with their rebelling muscles.

"We're going for a walk today, okay?" they might ask.

"No promises," the muscles responded. "You've been running me around for a lot of years. I need some time off!"

LORD, THIS IS FUNNY ON THE ONE HAND but all too true on the other. One day this week I noticed my mind was in gear but my knees were not! Thank You for reminding me to focus on what I have, rather than on what I don't have.

Take Note

Dear God:

I'm really glad I've learned the value of taking notes. I seem to need these reminders the older I get. That's why I keep a pad and pencil beside my recliner. As I think of what I need to do the next day, I jot it down before I forget or get distracted by a TV program or something in the newspaper.

As You know, I've long since given up on relying on my memory, although I read recently that if we want to improve and preserve our memories, we should consider taking up a musical instrument. Hmmm! Maybe I need to consider sitting down at the piano again. It's only been about 20 years since I last played!

Anyway, back to the notes. I went downstairs for my coffee this morning and found a note on the kitchen table. I wondered who had left it and whom it was for. Then it all hit home with thundering clarity and more than a dose of embarrassment.

"Remember to read notes from last night," it read. Sure enough, I had hastily scribbled this reminder before turning in last night. God is there any hope for me?

I LOVE IMAGINING THAT YOU ARE LAUGHING WITH ME, O LORD. I can almost feel Your gentle hand on my head reminding me that it's okay to remind myself not to forget and then to forget what I did to remind myself! You know what I need and You'll lead me to it—notepad or not.

ℒeftie!

Dear God:

My father is a hoot when I least expect it. On a good day, he knows me and responds to a dish of ice cream or a short ride around the nursing home in his wheelchair. On a bad day, I just stop by, say hello and good-bye, and kiss him on the cheek.

It's hard to watch him decline—especially since in his working days he was a very competent, highly regarded psychologist. As a child, I was amazed at his ability to analyze everything. He had an answer for every problem.

Maybe that's why he enjoys hanging around the nurses' station in the nursing home. It's a "happening" place—a whirl of activity to keep his mind and eyes engaged.

He's not very communicative anymore. I miss being able to have a conversation with him, but it's nearly impossible now. He has a hard time putting a full sentence together on the best of days.

Today I stopped by to see him and found him sitting in his usual spot, focused on the male nurse behind the counter. I spoke to him but he didn't respond. He seemed to be busy processing whatever had caught his attention.

He seemed intent on another male patient who appeared to be "fighting" the female nurse who was trying to give him a drink of juice.

Finally, Dad spoke up—without looking up: "You know what's wrong with him, don't you?" he bellowed.

The nurse lifted her eyes, perhaps anticipating his bit of wisdom. I glanced at Dad. "Tell us, Dad, what's wrong with him?" I asked.

"He's left-handed," he declared. Then Dad turned and wheeled himself down the hall. That was that! One more problem solved. Next?

LORD, WHAT FUN IT IS TO SEE OTHERS AND OURSELVES in a comical light. Most of us are too serious when a little laughter would do us more good than medicine. Come to think of it, You tell us in Scripture that "A cheerful heart is good medicine, but a crushed spirit dries up the bones" (Prov. 17:22).

Aromatic Socks

Dear God:

Would You please have a few private words with my husband about hygiene? He took off his socks the other evening before getting into bed and I nearly keeled over from the odor. I was about to run to the store and pick up a pair of Odor-Eaters, but it was too late to be out alone.

Instead, I told him—as politely as I could muster—to put his socks into the laundry basket. I'd tend to them first thing in the morning. He agreed since he was on his way to the bathroom anyway.

Off he went, socks in hand, but instead of dropping them into the clothes hamper, he absentmindedly dropped them into the toilet.

I wondered if I should come behind him with the laundry soap or simply flush them!

AREN'T WE A PAIR, O LORD! As we get older, we also get funnier. Maybe we could earn a few extra dollars as a couple of stand-up comics. That is if we can stay standing! It's good to laugh about such things. And I trust You are chuckling right along with us. It gladdens my heart to imagine You are.

What's in a Name?

Dear God:

Were You chuckling when You heard Lynda ask her friend Margaret to remind her of Mr. McCasland's wife's name? Lynda was obviously embarrassed; especially since the woman she was referring to was a former staff member at her church.

"I know her name as well as I know my own," Lynda told Margaret, exasperated at her sudden forgetfulness.

Margaret looked at her with a glint in her eye. "Her name is Linda!"

Lynda then replied, with chagrin, "Well, obviously I must be having trouble with my own name too!"

Oh, Lord, I've done something similar. I remember one day I was leading a group of travelers on a city tour and one of the tourists noted that my name tag was upside down. She seemed to be trying her best to figure it out so that she could call me by name!

I flushed with embarrassment, then quipped: "I always wear it this way—helps me remember who I am! But I'll turn it right side up for you, if you promise to help me out if I do forget my name!"

SOMETIMES, GOD, I JUST HAVE TO ROLL WITH IT. Senior moments are coming faster and more frequently these days.

Without a sense of humor, I don't think I could hold up my head! Maybe that's why it's best to hang out with people of my own kind. No one can point a finger at another, lest it come back to him or her a moment later. Thanks for being with me through them all.

Doing the Tan-Tan!

Dear God:

Remember when I was recovering from an injury and unable to get out in the sun for about two-and-a-half months? I thought I'd die. I love to be outdoors, so it was especially hard to obey the doctor's orders.

Then I thought about my visit to my sister and brother-in-law's house in the desert. I didn't want to stick out like a white flag with the Rancho Mirage golfing crowd. My husband agreed. I decided to treat myself to a self-tan treatment. *Just the ticket,* I thought, *then I won't feel so self-conscious.*

For three days in a row before we left, I applied the tanning cream to my arms, neck and upper chest area twice a day. I loved working at my computer while still getting a tan! *I could get used to this,* I thought.

"Yes, I'm getting tanner by the day and definitely looking better," I told myself each evening before bed.

The day we were to leave, I took a few moments to pack my overnight case. I wanted to throw in some sunscreen, but I couldn't find it anywhere. That seemed odd. I was sure I had purchased it at the same time I bought the self-tanning cream. In fact, both products came in a similar-looking squeeze tube.

I put on my glasses to get a better look at what I had been applying for the past three days. Oh no! I had been using sunscreen instead of self-tanning cream.

Next stop? The optometrist! I definitely needed a new pair of glasses. How could I have considered myself more tan after two days of using sunscreen? Am I at that point in life where I only see what I want to see? Not good!

GOD, HELP ME, PLEASE, to see what You want me to see—in myself as well as in the world around me—and most importantly let me see You in all things.

Spray Away!

Dear God:

There I was about to take the stage and wow the crowd with my message! But first a quick visit to the ladies' room to check my lipstick and mascara and put any stray hairs in place. A little spray would do the trick. Even a stiff breeze couldn't ruffle my tresses after that!

I opened my purse, sprayed here and sprayed there. Wait a minute. Something was wrong. Instead of holding my hair in place, the entire "do" collapsed into wet strands.

I looked at the small bottle in my hand. I was ready to pitch it out the sixteenth story window of the hotel. So much for my $20 coiffure—not yet 24-hours old. I was indignant as I looked in the mirror—ready to return to the drug store and demand my money back. Then I glanced at the label on the spray bottle. It was cologne.

I smelled "real good" that day—but I didn't look too swift!

And to top it off, a woman in the audience came up to me after my presentation. It was clear she had a few words of encouragement for me after listening to my lament over the state of my hair.

"You may not be the most attractive thing on the block," she said, "but you're a good speaker!"

I TOOK HER WORDS AND RAN. God, is this the price of fame? One minute the world loves you and the next you're done for! Actually, yes, that is the way it is in the world. Yet You remind me to live in the world, not to be of it (see Rom. 12:2; 1 John 2:15). I think I'll take Your advice—thank You very much.

To Brush or Not to Brush

Dear God:

When am I going to get this straight? I walk into the bathroom intent on brushing my teeth, but then I notice the towels need laundering, so I carry them to the washing machine. I return to the bathroom because something unfinished is on my mind. I see my toothbrush and wonder aloud, "Have I already brushed this morning?"

I check the drinking glass and there's a bit of water left in it. But that could be from rinsing my mouth after taking my allergy pill. Next I touch the toothbrush. If it's wet I know I've brushed; if it's dry I haven't. But then again . . . Oh, to heck with it, I'll brush just to be on the safe side. I just hope I can remember this time, or I'll spend my day in the bathroom wearing out my teeth!

What a state of affairs, dear God. Has it come to this? I can't even remember the simple little routines of daily life? I'm a goner if I can't keep up with basic hygiene practices. Actually, it's pretty funny when I think more about it. I'll either be in line for gingivitis treatment (for lack of brushing) or up for an award for the most gleaming teeth in the neighborhood.

GOD, YOU ARE SO GOOD TO ME. I feel Your tender love and Your loving tenderness when I make these silly mistakes.

I'm so glad You are not frowning and groaning at me at this stage of my life—like *some* people I know (who shall remain nameless)!

Unlisted!

Dear God:

If only I were as organized as Don. He has all his ducks in a row—shoes, socks, shirts, tools, toys and tacks! No wonder you put us together. I am learning after 40 years of marriage the benefit of keeping things in order. I see how little time he spends looking for lost items because he knows where they are.

I'm another story. My shoes, socks and shirts are . . . well, I'm not sure where they are. They're around here somewhere. I look for them only when I need them.

Don's tidy ways even spill over into the realm of paper. He has a neatly typed list of names and phone numbers of friends and family members for us to take on the road when we travel. And we travel a lot, if you don't know.

As we prepared for our latest trip with our motor-home caravan, I was busy packing food, clothing and personal items. Don, in the meantime, assembled the necessary paper items: checkbook, shopping list, maps.

The morning of our departure, he went over the list of phone numbers and addresses to be sure it was current. Just then the phone rang. While talking, Don needed both hands to find some information for the caller, so he set down the list on top of our paper shredder. A corner of the page slipped into the paper slot and suddenly the machine began gobbling the sheet before Don realized what he had done.

When he heard the motor humming, he frantically grabbed for the page and jerked it upward, lifting the entire shredder off the floor! Quickly, he pushed the reverse button and salvaged at least part of the page. The top of his special typed list looked like the Jetson kid's spiked hair.

Poor Don! He has been so attentive to our papers and possessions, keeping every one in pristine condition and perfect order. And he's proud of it! He also wishes I would learn from his example.

DEAR GOD, I HAVE TO ADMIT I chuckled a bit—behind my hand, of course. Even *Don* can make a mistake, I mused! Of course, it's always more fun to laugh at someone else's senior moments than to smile at my own.

Caller ID

Dear God:

My kids keep telling me that I need caller ID. They feel that I let salespeople take advantage of me by catching me off-guard at dinnertime or when I'm hurrying out the door. They don't want me to buy stuff I don't need or to donate to questionable charities.

I don't think I need it. What do You think, Lord? I believe there's an extra charge for it as well. But it's not only the money; I don't want to know ahead of time who's calling. I like to be surprised. That's part of the fun of receiving phone calls. I'm never sure who's on the other end! And I enjoy talking to people—even if a few of them are only interested in selling me something or getting my response to a survey.

But I do wish someone would come up with a plan or a gadget that would tell me who *I'm* calling, since half of the time I dial a number and before the person answers, I've forgotten who I've called. Now there's a senior moment. How embarrassing is that? In two seconds the person's name drops right out of my mind.

So far no one has pitched such a product or service to me. Meanwhile, I use my own version—a simple notebook with a list of everyone who calls and everyone I call—including their full name, phone number, and the time and date we talked or the time and date they left a message.

In some cases, however, I can see the benefits of caller ID for *other* people. Like the day I called the hair salon for an appointment for a haircut. All the stylists were booked. The receptionist said she'd phone me if there were a cancellation.

"Would you verify your phone number for me?" she asked.

I gave it to her.

Then she had the nerve to ask me if I was sure that was the correct number. I was insulted.

"Yes, it's my number," I snapped. "I've had it for 20 years."

"Well, that's not the number I show on the caller ID," the woman said politely.

"Uh . . . better go with the caller ID," I said.

See what I mean, God? You might be smiling at my funny antics, but I'm not! They are downright humiliating sometimes! Fortunately, some people are kind enough to remind me of my senior moments without thoroughly debilitating me. Certainly that's true of You and I thank You for it.

LORD, WHEN I CALL YOU, or You call me, there is no mistaking Your voice. You know Your sheep and they know You. How wonderful to have this certainty.

High Time for Tea

Dear God:

This afternoon I invited a new neighbor for tea. I remembered Your teaching about hospitality. This seemed like the perfect opportunity to practice it. Now that I'm a senior, I tend to do things as simply as possible. One of my time-saving tricks is to make tea in my coffeemaker!

Shortly before Betty's arrival, I carefully cleaned the glass carafe, placed a mandarin orange spice tea bag in it, sat it on the base, filled the top with the appropriate amount of water and flipped it on.

Then I placed a paper doily, two of my antique bone china cups and saucers, and a small plate of freshly baked cookies on a serving tray.

Betty arrived and I served her while we got acquainted. As I raised my cup, I noticed the tea didn't have the same orange aroma I was used to, and when I sipped it, it had an unfamiliar flavor. I let it go since we were in the midst of conversation.

Betty drained her cup and after exchanging a few more pleasantries, she thanked me for the visit and headed for the door.

After my new friend left, I examined the coffee pot and, yes, Lord—you guessed it—I had left the morning coffee grounds in the filter basket. Have you ever tasted coffee-flavored tea? I don't recommend it.

The next day I confessed to Betty what I had done and apologized. We had a good laugh. I haven't made that mistake since. And she's agreed to give me another chance!

LORD, SOME OF THESE MOMENTS ARE FUNNY and some are humiliating. I'm so glad You don't hold them against me, but instead smile right along with me, knowing that I can always use a dose of humility and a bit of humor as well.

Charge It!

Dear God:

This stunt takes the cake for sure. Today I walked up to the ATM at my local bank, pulled out a plastic card and inserted it into the slot—or tried to. It wouldn't budge. I turned it around and pushed again. Still no response. I was in a hurry and felt myself getting impatient.

My money is in there, I thought to myself. *Since when does the bank have the right to keep me from withdrawing my own funds? I'm going to have a word with the manager about this.*

Before storming into the bank, however, I decided to insert the card one more time, this time slowly and deliberately, in case something was out of balance or off-track.

Still no results. I put the card back in my wallet and marched into the bank ready for a fistfight if necessary. I handed the card to the manager and stated in a firm tone, "Mr. Green, something is wrong with your ATM. It will not take my bank card, yet it took the one from the client just before me. What is going on? I need answers and I need them right now. I'm in a hurry."

Mr. Green took my card, glanced at it and then looked at me with a twinkle in his eye. "Ma'am, there's nothing wrong with our ATM machine or your card. This card will work just fine for charging your purchases at Penney's."

I dropped my head in embarrassment, thanked him for his time and walked out of the bank feeling as if the entire world was looking at me. I put the Penney's charge card back in my wallet, and this time pulled out my ATM card, inserted it and withdrew the cash I needed. I was off to my appointment within seconds, hopefully a bit wiser and a lot more humble.

THANK YOU, LORD, FOR SHOWING ME what a fool I can be when I rush to judgment about another person or institution. When I think of this situation, I realize how quickly I found fault with someone else. I didn't even take a moment to check myself, to see if perhaps I had made a mistake. I automatically put the blame on another. Help me today to slow down, breathe deeply and ask You for help when I feel confounded or confused.

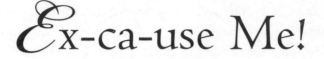Ex-ca-use Me!

Dear God:

I really put my foot in my mouth today. I was so excited about seeing my new grandchild that I didn't stop to inquire about my son-in-law, Daniel, when I came to visit. I just strode right down the hall eager to meet little Peter, my daughter, Rita, a step behind.

Then suddenly there was Daniel—naked as a jaybird. He had just stepped out of the bathroom after taking a shower. The sound of the pelting water kept him from hearing me coming down the hall. We were both embarrassed. I screamed and covered my eyes as Daniel dashed into the bedroom and slammed the door.

Rita broke up laughing and my face must have turned red. It sure felt hot! I didn't know what to say or do. It would have been best if I just let it go. Mistakes happen. It's not as though I had never seen a man's nude body before!

But You know me, Lord. I like to make peace and be sure everyone is happy and congenial. When Daniel came into the living room moments later fully dressed and smiling, I was determined to make him comfortable.

"That's alright, Daniel," I said apologetically. "I've seen a lot worse than that!"

Ooooh! Lord, I goofed big time! But Daniel was gracious. We laughed it off and he did hug me good-bye when it was time to leave.

SOMETIMES THE BEST WAY TO FIX a sticky situation is to drop it. And sometimes it's best to acknowledge it and admit our fault. But I'm really glad You don't drop it when I do something silly or stupid or thoughtless. You keep on teaching me until I get it. Thank You for Your patience with me.

Soufflé Surprise

Dear God:

Today for lunch I had my heart and taste buds set on finishing off the spinach soufflé I made yesterday. All I needed to do was warm it up a bit, so I placed it in the microwave oven.

While waiting I made a ham and cheese sandwich with lots of lettuce and a slice of tomato. I topped off my savory lunch with a tall glass of chocolate milk. Wait! What about dessert? I always have room for one little cookie, so I reached into the cookie jar and took out a lemon wafer. I looked forward to putting all the items on a tray and going outside to eat in the garden. I did just that.

When I finished I walked into the kitchen, washed up the few dishes I used and returned to my reading. Something preyed on my mind, but I didn't know what it was, so I let it go. My mind isn't as sharp as it used to be. I figured if it was important it would come back to me.

Sure enough, the next morning it did come back. I opened the microwave oven to heat some water for instant coffee and there sat my serving of spinach soufflé—dried out and dreary looking.

LORD, IT'S A GOOD THING You've told us not to be anxious about what we eat or drink, because life is more than food. But still, I'd like to think that I can keep it together enough to remember to take out what I put into the microwave when it's ready—not a day later!

A Must-See Movie

Dear God:

I love the movies, I have to admit. A good story with drama, action, some love interest and an intriguing plot that inspires and entertains is just what I look for when I want to spend an afternoon at the cinema.

I like to talk about films with friends too. We trade stories and opinions about what's hot and what's not and then recommend our favorites or pan the ones we don't like.

As I get older, however, it's getting more and more difficult to keep the names and story lines straight. The more time that passes between films, the less apt I am to remember what I want to share with a friend.

That happened the other day. My friend Jane likes historical fiction, so I was sure she'd enjoy one of my favorite movies. But as I started to tell her about it, I couldn't recall the title. So I did the next best thing. I decided to name the female lead, but I couldn't think of her name either. Then I tried to think of the name of the man she's married to, but his name escaped my memory as well. Surely I could recall his sister, because she was a famous actress a couple of decades ago and recently she's become a book author.

Well, neither of us got very far in the conversation because every time I tried to nail a detail, it dropped out of my mind.

Finally, I gave up and promised to call her when all that information came back—even if it was at three o'clock in the morning!

Sure enough, the next day I remembered that the female lead's name is Annette Bening who is married to Warren Beatty whose sister is Shirley MacLaine, but I still couldn't pull the title of the film. So I drove over to the video rental store in my neighborhood and asked for help.

The clerk, at least 40 years my junior, couldn't remember it either, though he seemed to know the movie I was referring to. He then pulled out a book listing all the films available on video within the last two years. We checked under Annette Bening's name, but the list did not include the movie I was looking for—at least I don't think it did. But then come to think of it, if I didn't know the name, how could I expect to recognize it on a printed list?

GOD, I HAVE NOT YET CALLED MY FRIEND, nor will I until I can solve this mystery once and for all! Is this a senior moment or what? Must I now take a notepad and pen with me to the movies? (And, of course, a flashlight.)

$\mathscr{L}$icense to Kill

Dear God:

Only You know the true story—how much trouble I've had over the years with the Department of Motor Vehicles. We've moved around so much that I can't keep one state's rules and regulations straight from another's. They're making me crazy!

Remember what happened in Oregon? All I wanted to do was exchange an item at a store. The salesperson asked to see my driver's license for proof of identity! What was that about? I wasn't even making a purchase. I dug out the license and slapped it on the counter in front of her. She looked at me, then at the license, then back at me again. With a raised eyebrow she spoke in a judgmental tone. "It appears your license has expired."

Needless to say, I slunk out of the store, afraid to drive home. What if I got pulled over? The next day I called the DMV and asked the clerk to check my standing. Sure enough, I had been driving illegally for a year and a half.

"Because your license has expired," the woman announced, "you'll need to come in for a written test, an eye test and a road test."

My stomach churned at just the thought of what that would entail. But I worried for nothing because I passed the written and eye tests without a hitch. The road test was another matter.

As the driving officer and I left the parking lot, he instructed me to turn left and go down a main street in the small town of Roseburg. I remember my mind spinning. Suddenly I couldn't think of which was left and which was right. I turned the wheel first one way and then the other before I made the full turn.

Then I drove the length of the street feeling pretty proud of myself and also grateful that it was early in the morning and there was little traffic. The officer waved at people he knew and then motioned for me to return to the motor vehicle center.

As I pulled up to the curb, I got scared. I noticed him putting little check marks on the form attached to his clipboard. I asked if I needed to sign anything, feeling certain I had passed and would soon be on my way.

"Not today, ma'am," he said. "You just drove the length of a one-way street the wrong way. If the traffic had been heavy, you could have killed us both."

I wouldn't be driving again any time soon!

Over the years, I've won a few and lost a few. I'm losing again. I just checked my license last night. It's expired!

LORD, WHAT IS WITH these senior moments when it comes to my driving? Will I ever get this straight? Or will I arrive at heaven's gate and be asked to show my driver's license to prove I belong there? I think I'll let You do the driving from now on. It's a lot safer with You behind the wheel of my life.

Salmon Drop

Dear God:

I was so looking forward to taking a slab of the cooked salmon I had made for dinner last night in my lunch on the trail. But when I started assembling my pack, I couldn't find the fish anywhere. I was sure I had put it in the refrigerator. That would make the most sense—to keep it fresh and cool. I looked there. Nope—not on any of the shelves!

I wondered if I had put it in my pack without thinking. I wouldn't put it past me with all that was on my mind that week. But it wasn't there either.

The trash? Could I have dropped it in there with the leftovers I didn't want to save? Pretty silly if I did, but hey, I had to check all the possibilities. Not there either.

God, this was beginning to get to me. A real mystery. The more I looked through the motor home, the more frustrated I became. I just knew that salmon was here somewhere.

Finally, I did what I should have done in the first place—turned it over to You. And voilà! You led me right to it. It had dropped between the end of the countertop and the trash container.

But it was too late. I had to throw it away and settle for a peanut-butter-and-jelly sandwich! By the time we stopped for lunch on the trail, I was so hungry it really didn't matter what I had to eat.

THANK YOU FOR THE FOOD YOU PROVIDE, whatever it is. As the beautiful old hymn reminds me, "All that I have Your hand hath provided. Great is Your faithfulness, O Lord."*

* Thomas O. Chisholm, "Great Is Thy Faithfulness," © 1923, 1951 Hope Publishing Company.

$\mathscr{S}$tiff Upper Lip

Dear God:

I'd sure appreciate it if You'd remind my daughter of Your commandment to honor her father and mother. Here I am reaching obsolescence with its imploding hormones just as Katrina reaches adolescence with its exploding hormones. We're not doing too well—neither one of us.

My own changes are hard enough. They seem to have snuck up on me with all their humiliating effects, including a shadowed upper lip. I feel like a teenager as I hide out in the bathroom trying to stay ahead of my unwanted crop.

I admit that sometimes I get behind, like this afternoon when I picked up Katrina from school.

"Mom," she said, looking at me with a deep and concerned expression.

Lord, I thought for sure she was entertaining profound thoughts and was ready for one of those heart-to-heart, mother-daughter talks since we were alone in the car.

"Yes, sweet pie," I replied, ready to pour forth motherly wisdom.

"How come you have whiskers?" she asked bluntly.

My secret's out, I thought, *my femininity threatened.*

"Because I'm about to take a second career as the bearded lady at the circus," I snapped.

The eyes that once read the fine print on a pill bottle cannot even see the whiskers on her own face with a magnifying mirror! I admit it. I need help. Maybe I can get Katrina on my side by asking her to check me out each morning before I show up in public! Now there's a thought. I'll turn her into an advocate instead of an enemy of my inevitable aging and all that goes with it.

LORD, ONLY YOU KNOW that I'm often laughing on the outside but crying on the inside. It's not fun to grow older. Maybe what I need is to renew my mind, embracing whatever You send my way, even the "hairy" experiences.

Face-to-Face

Dear God:

What do You think of this? My wife decided to check the faucet washer attached to the kitchen sink sprayer hose. Sometimes the nozzle gets clogged and needs a good cleaning. But instead of holding it over the sink, she held it in such a way that it was pointed directly at me. I was standing by to assist if needed.

When she was finished, she turned on the faucet to rinse her hands. Without realizing it, she rinsed my face as well!

But that was not the last of my unfortunate experiences that day. For two hours I hunted for the keys to my car. The bedroom, kitchen, bathroom and living room would not surrender them. The front and backseat of the car failed to turn them over to me.

Finally, feeling defeated and disgusted, I gave in and decided to walk to the store. *The exercise will do me good*, I told myself, trying to retrieve a bit of positive energy. I put my hands into my coat pocket to fish out the house key so I could lock the front door.

Sure enough, as the saying goes, What you're looking for will always be in the last place you look—or feel!

FUNNY HOW THESE THINGS CAN GET TO ME, even though they've become a part of my life as a senior. Next time, nudge me, O Lord, to check with You first. You always know where everything is and You always look out for my best interest.

Part 2:
Surprising
Moments

$\mathcal{R}$IP

Dear God:

You know how much I enjoy camping. It's always a treat to go to the Sierras for a week of hiking, relaxing by the campfire at night and cooking "vittles" over an open fire. Thank You for Your gift of nature and for all the critters—from bears to crickets!

My grandchildren love my stories about the bears our group has encountered. But this year I had a different story to tell.

One morning as I reached for my breakfast food in the back of my station wagon, I noticed that several of the plastic bags had holes in them. One in particular was badly punctured. It had been filled with various nuts and dried fruits. When I picked it up, most of the contents fell out.

That's strange, I thought to myself. *I'm sure I put this mix in a brand-new zippered bag.* "Oh well, I'll deal with this later," I muttered.

It was time for our morning hike and I didn't want to be late. When we returned that afternoon, I opened my car to take out a snack and some water, and I noticed several other bags were also punctured. Even my tissues were perforated. I assumed it was an insect and let it go. Flies and mosquitoes outnumbered us, so I just chalked it up to life in the outdoors!

Several days later we broke camp and said our good-byes. Then I drove down the mountain into town to the motel where I planned to spend the night before heading home the following day.

I organized my gear, did a couple of loads of laundry, ate dinner and headed for bed. The next morning when I opened my car a terrible stench hit my nose! *What is that about?* I wondered. I didn't have any fresh food in the car, so I was really puzzled.

Then suddenly I noticed a small furry creature curled up in a little open box I had left on the floor of the backseat. A long tail hung over the edge. A field mouse! Eeek! I shivered at the sight. Poor fella must have sneaked in when my car was open and then died in the extreme heat of the day after I locked up my car.

"Help!" I called to one of the employees at the motel. "A dead mouse. I can't bear to touch him. Would you please remove him for me?"

The man chuckled, reached in and carried the little guy, box and all, to the trash container. I thanked him and off he went.

But then I had a shame attack. It was just a field mouse for heaven's sake. Why did I make such a big deal out of it? After all, he was one of God's creatures, as much as I am. Surely I could afford to allow him to help himself to a few nuts and berries. I had more food than I'd ever eat in a week.

It was my fault for not keeping my things better concealed and for leaving my car door open as I trotted back and forth in the campground.

It was a senior moment, alright. An unforgettable one!

LORD, YOU TAUGHT ME SOMETHING BEAUTIFUL THAT DAY. You showed me the importance of treating all of Your creation with love and respect. Just as You care for me, You also care for the lilies of the field and the birds of the air and the mice of the field.

$\mathcal{H}$itchhiker

Dear God:

I am notorious for my lack of direction in the wilderness. Just today I got to see again that I cannot even go off-trail for a two-minute "bush break" without getting lost.

How embarrassing! I told my hiking buddies I'd be right back. They said they'd start up the trail and I could catch up. They'd walk slowly, so I wouldn't be far behind.

When I finished, however, I couldn't remember where to walk to hit the trailhead. It had been so easy to leave the trail. Why did it seem so difficult to find it again?

I turned in the direction I thought was correct, but I ran into more trees. I turned again and headed back to where I started, but I still couldn't find the right spot. Suddenly a forest of trees and shrubs surrounded me with no trail in sight.

I panicked. I called out but no one answered. A moment later I heard the sound of an engine. *I'll just follow it till I reach the road,* I thought. But once the vehicle passed, I was surrounded by silence except for the occasional flapping of a bird's wings. Still no road.

By this time I was shaking with fear and tears spilled down my cheeks. I kept walking, praying I'd come across someone who could help. Suddenly, miraculously, I was standing on blacktop. I stood at the edge of the road and stuck out my hand, hoping to flag down a motorcycle, horseback rider, driver, any-one who could show me where to go.

From a distance I heard the roar of a semitruck barreling down the highway. I stuck out my hand and waved frantically, breathing so hard by then I thought my lungs would burst.

The driver stopped. "Oh, thank God," I whispered. I tossed aside any thoughts of fear or caution about talking to or hitching rides with strangers. I was just so glad to see another human being!

"You look like you need some help," the man said, smiling. "What can I do for you?"

"I've lost track of my hiking friends," I said in a small voice. "I'm not even sure where the trailhead is. I was supposed to meet them there."

"Hey, I can fix that," he said. "I just saw a group of hikers back there a mile or so. I'll run you back."

I hopped in and off we went. A minute or so later I caught sight of my fellow hikers huddled at the trailhead where they had returned when I didn't show up.

Everyone hugged me and said how relieved they were that I was safe. I waved to the driver as he zoomed off.

The next time I need a "bush break," I'll take a buddy with me!

LORD, THANK YOU FOR PROVIDING A TRAVEL ANGEL in the nick of time. I'm reminded again of Your promise to protect me when I'm in trouble and to show me when to turn right and when to turn left. I simply need to ask and You are there.

Lunch Box Leftovers

Dear God:

Angie, Marge, Lucy and I had our usual monthly get-together over lunch. It's always a hoot to be with these gals, especially Angie. Half the time I'm not sure she knows which way is "up," but she sure is fun to be around. I always feel better after spending time with her.

Well, this month topped all the others. After lunch we each asked for a take-out container for our leftovers. Angie said she looked forward to having hers for dinner since her husband had a meeting that night and wouldn't be home till late.

As we said good-bye and hugged one another, I noticed Angie place her container on top of her car while she fumbled in her purse for her keys—something she did regularly.

My car was parked next to hers, so I followed her out of the parking lot. As I stopped at the exit, I noticed her food container was still on top of her car. I beeped at her, but she didn't respond. She turned successfully without losing her lunch! It slid a bit but stayed on top. I couldn't believe it. I started laughing. This was so like Angie.

We continued down the street to the stoplight at the next corner. I honked again. Then Marge did the same as she came up beside me and motioned to the box on top of Angie's car. We both giggled.

Then suddenly the light turned green and Angie lurched forward. That did it. The box of leftover lasagna fell off the car and spilled onto the street. Drivers started honking their horns, people shouted through open windows, trying to get Angie's attention. Nothing worked. Off she went, oblivious of the traffic jam she had created.

I drove home, chuckling to myself, wondering what Angie would think when she arrived home without her leftover lunch. I didn't have the heart to tell her what happened! Maybe I will next month when we meet.

LORD, WE ARE SUCH FUNNY CREATURES. We are "out to lunch" in so many areas of life. Good thing You are there to clean up the mess and to whisper words of encouragement when we get ourselves in a jam.

$\mathscr{P}$urse Snatcher

Dear God:

You heard me talk about Angie yesterday. I'm back today to tell You the latest. She called to let me know that she had put her purse—you guessed it—on top of her car while she juggled some groceries and fumbled for her keys. Then she got in the car and drove off.

When she arrived home, she realized her purse was not in its usual place in the front seat, passenger side. She panicked, but then remembered the last time she saw it, it was on top of the car. Disaster! It was probably lying somewhere on the highway, or worse yet, someone may have picked it up and stolen her money and credit cards.

Angie called the local police station and miracle of miracles, the officer who answered said someone had just phoned in to report that he had found a purse on the highway, snatched it up when the traffic slowed, and would drop by with it that afternoon.

Long story short—Angie got her purse back. That is so like her, dear Lord. She lives by the seat of her pants, but it seems to work.

This reminds me of the time I left two books on top of my car. I was in such a rush that day and my arms were so full that I didn't know what to take care of first. So I put the books on the roof of the car, got in and sped away. To this day I have no idea where or when they fell off. I never heard a thing; I was so intent on getting to my destination.

I hope whoever found them enjoyed a good read.

WE ARE SO BLESSED that You take care of us no matter what. Senior moments don't faze You, dear God. You just love us and chuckle right along with us when we make these innocent and unthinking mistakes. Thank You that in the Bible You remind us that You are our hiding place, our high tower, our rock and refuge (see Ps. 18:2, *KJV*).

Lost and Found

Dear God:

My wife and I just spent an hour searching for my wallet—in the weeds, along the curb, up and down the street, and all over the parking lot in front of the movie theater where we just watched a film.

What a bummer! We went from the theater to the coffee shop, and when I reached for my money, my wallet was gone. I know I had it in my back pocket—where I always keep it. *Or did I leave it at home?* I wondered.

It was a sad ending to a happy date with my wife. Finally we came home and just gave it up to You. What more could we do? We planned on calling all the card companies on Monday and making arrangements for a new driver's license and so on.

And then, O God, You came through in a most astounding way—right in the middle of my senior moment. A phone message was waiting for me. A man had called to say he found my wallet in the theater by his feet and had taken it home and called right away, knowing the owner would probably be frantic.

I returned his call immediately and told him I wanted to give him a $50 reward. He was ecstatic. His wife needed dental care and it would cost $50!

LORD, HOW GRACIOUS YOU ARE! I never would have imagined that You'd use my mistake to be a blessing to someone else. I'm going to stay on my toes from now on, watching for what You will do next!

$\mathscr{S}$tood Up!

Dear God:

Imagine how I felt last night when my wife stood me up for a date that she initiated! I agreed with her that we had not been spending enough time together, so we decided to set aside every Tuesday evening from that point on for a movie, a concert, dinner, a walk or coffee and dessert.

I have to admit I liked the idea, and I really looked forward to our "first" date. I offered to get the ball rolling. After work the following Tuesday, I invited Maureen to dinner at one of our favorite spots, Foster's Grille. We agreed to meet there in an hour.

I completed the work on my desk and then hurried over to the restaurant, determined not to be late this time. I arrived just two minutes after the hour—proud of myself for making the effort. Maureen was nowhere in sight. *Aha*, I thought. *This time she's late. I'll have to razz her for a change.*

After 20 minutes of pacing the parking lot, it didn't seem funny anymore. I walked around the building several times, but I did not see her car. I went inside, checked at the desk and asked someone to go into the ladies' room and call her name. Nothing. Nada. Maureen was not there.

I grabbed my cell phone and called her. By then I was beginning to imagine all sorts of things.

"I'm at Foster's, as we agreed," she said, a touch of annoyance in her voice. "I'm standing right here next to the handicapped parking spot in front."

I was baffled. I was standing there, myself, looking at the only two handicapped spaces near the restaurant, and she was clearly not beside me.

"I can't imagine how I've missed you," I said, bewildered. "Boy, I must be losing it," I muttered. "I'll check to see if I'm in the wrong spot." We hung up and I dashed around the facility once more. No car. No Maureen. My patience was running out.

I returned to my truck, picked up my cell phone from the seat where I'd left it and dialed her again.

"Hi, honey," she responded in a sheepish voice. "Did you get the voice-mail message I just sent you?"

"No," I barked. "I've been running around this restaurant trying to find you. What is going on? Is this some kind of joke?"

"I'm so sorry," she said. "I'm standing next to the handicapped parking space, but I'm at Fuddruckers instead of Foster's. I guess I had that name in my mind, so I drove here without thinking."

"I'll be right over," I said. "Don't move." I didn't dare suggest she come and meet me!

We sat down to dinner—finally—at 9:00 P.M., starved and grumpy. After a few bites of food, we were both ready to forgive one another and to enjoy what was left of our first Tuesday night date. By the time we finished eating, we were both yawning. We went straight home and fell into bed laughing. We decided that the following week we'd drive to our destination together, so we could actually spend the evening *with* one another!

OH LORD, DOES THIS SOUND FAMILIAR? How many times do I make a date to spend time with You and then fail to show up? I'm going to use this experience as a reminder to plan, to listen and to follow through whether it's a date with my wife or a date with You.

$\mathcal{C}$ar Thief

Dear God:

What do you think of this story found in a Florida newspaper? It's enough to make me sit up and take notice!

An elderly lady went shopping in the mall. Upon returning to her car she caught sight of four men trying to take her vehicle. She would have none of that. Never mind that she was over 70 and they were strong young males, less than half her age.

She dropped her shopping bags and drew her handgun, and then proceeded to scream at the top of her voice, "I have a gun, and I know how to use it! Get out of the car—*now!*"

The four men didn't wait for a second invitation. They jumped out and ran as fast as they could. The woman, somewhat shaken, loaded her shopping bags into the back of the car and slid into the driver's seat. She was so nervous she couldn't get her key into the ignition. She tried again and again—until it suddenly dawned on her why it wasn't working.

She got out of the car, walked up and down the aisle, and finally found her own car parked four or five spaces away. She loaded her bags into her car and then drove straight to the police station.

She told the sergeant her story and he nearly fell over he laughed so hard. Then he pointed to the other end of the counter, where four young men were reporting a carjacking by a mad, elderly woman described as white, less than five-feet tall, with curly white hair, wearing glasses and carrying a large handgun.

No charges were filed! Instead, they all had a good laugh together.

I'M GLAD TO KNOW IT TURNED OUT alright for everyone involved. In today's unpredictable world you never know what's going to happen next, especially when a gun or a car is in the mix. Thank you that your Holy Spirit can turn things around in the nick of time—especially when we think we know the truth—even when we don't.

*O*ops!

Dear God:

Thank you for letting Mom stay with me till she was 92. What a blessing that was. I still miss her, but I know she's happy in heaven with you. Today I'm thinking about all the Sundays we shared with one another after Dad died. We decided to take turns attending services at each other's churches. I remember one Sunday in particular—when I had a senior moment big time. I never did tell Mom about it, so I guess I'm writing about it here so that I can let go of it. I feel guilty about what I did that day.

At the time, Mom lived on the fifth floor of a high-rise senior apartment. I'd call her from home each Sunday morning just before I left, and by the time I arrived, she'd be waiting at the main entrance.

That Sunday, however, I had my mind on other things—a challenge at work, a problem at home. Suddenly, I pulled into the parking lot of Mom's church and realized I was alone. I had forgotten to pick her up. How terrible. *The poor woman is probably standing there worried about me*, I thought. I knew then I had to break down and buy each of us a cell phone.

Quickly, I backed out of my parking place and whizzed the five miles to Mother's. Sure enough, there she was, waiting by the entrance. I hopped out of the car and kissed her, then opened the passenger door.

"My gosh, but that took you a long time," she said. "Are you alright? I was beginning to worry."

"Well, you know how traffic can be on a Sunday morning," I lied.

"Just so you're safe," she said, and patted my hand.

Shame on me, God, for not telling the truth, but how could I admit to my mother that I had forgotten her?

Oops! Now she knows. Lord, would you mind putting in a good word for me?

LORD, I AM AMAZED at how quick I am to cover my tracks, to fib, to fudge, to just plain lie when I'm too embarrassed to admit the truth. Or is it my pride? I don't like to be caught looking foolish. Help me, God, to overcome this trait and to be the human being you created me to be—someone who can be transparent even when I've made an honest mistake.

ℒunch Bunch

Dear God:

I invited my bridge group for lunch. It was my turn, and I was ready for it. I had a great recipe for a special salad, and I was in the mood to make a luscious dessert. The ladies love their sweets.

I set the date and put in on my calendar: June 14 at noon.

Everyone responded affirmatively. There'd be eight of us in all. I really got into the planning, preparing and decorating. I gave myself plenty of time to get my house in order, polish the silver and wash my good china, which I rarely use now that Barney's gone.

Then it happened. On June 4 at 11:50 A.M. the doorbell rang. Three ladies appeared on the doorstep and within a moment or two the remaining four drove up in Jane's wagon.

I was floored! "I'm sorry," I apologized. "It's so nice of you to stop by. But look at me; I'm a mess. I was in the garden all morning."

Janet stepped forward. "We're here for the June luncheon," she said with a bewildered look on her face. "Is something wrong?"

Wrong? Well, sure, you've got the wrong date, I wanted to shout—but of course I didn't. These were my good friends.

Miriam pulled out her invitation and passed it to me. There circled in red was the date and time for the luncheon at *my* house! Plain as day it said, "June 4 at noon." I ran into the kitchen without saying a word and grabbed my calendar off the wall. The date

I had circled was June 14, not June 4. I was in shock. How could that be?

I invited the ladies inside and we all laughed about this curious predicament. We never did figure out what happened. The closest I could come to a logical explanation was that when I typed in the date, my fingers flew over the keyboard so fast that I missed typing in the number 1 in front of the 4.

So much for my lovely plans for a leisurely luncheon at my house. I told my friends to hang out for a minute while I changed clothes. Ten minutes later I walked into the living room and announced plan B.

"Come on, ladies," I said. "We're going to Patty's Café. Lunch is on me!"

GOD, THIS WAS A COSTLY WAY TO turn a senior moment into a spontaneous moment. I'll probably never live it down, but more important, we had fun, the food was great and everyone applauded me for being a good sport!

Safety in Numbers

Dear God:

Yesterday I was so proud of myself. I finally got our "papers" organized and all the clutter cleared out. I told Jim I'd take the important stuff to the safe-deposit box at Community Bank. He had opened an account some time ago, but until today we didn't have things in enough order to use it.

He was thrilled not to have to deal with this and thanked me with a hug as he left for work. "I'll check in with you later, hon," he said as he walked out the door.

It took a few minutes to locate the key. I found it in the top drawer of Jim's desk with a gazillion other loose keys and paper clips. *When will that man get it together?* I wondered, feeling self-righteous now that I had done my part.

Finally I was dressed, key in hand, glasses on nose, car keys in purse, car in garage! It's come to the point where I have to do a personal "check" whenever I go somewhere or I'm bound to leave something behind. Today was no exception.

I jumped in the car and drove directly to the bank so that I could get this chore past me. I parked, walked into the bank and looked for the vault. I didn't see it where I had remembered, so I assumed it had been moved. But for the life of me I couldn't imagine how one moves a bank vault!

I asked a teller to let me in. She looked at me quizzically as I handed her my identification and showed her my safe-deposit box key. "We don't have boxes here," she said. "Perhaps you have one at another bank. There are several different banks here in Bay Crest," she said.

At that point, I wanted to punch her lights out. She looked at me as though I were a pathetic, little old lady who had no clue where she was or how she got there. Actually, she might have been right. I started feeling exactly like that.

I walked out of the bank, anxious and confused. Jim had told me specifically that he had opened a box at Community Bank. There was only one branch in our town. *What was going on?* I wondered.

I grabbed my cell phone and called him at work. I admit I was not polite. Alright, I was rude and loud.

In a quiet voice, full of apology, he told me what happened. The day he opened the account for a safe-deposit box, he was at work. "I noticed a branch of Community Bank in the shopping mall on First Avenue," he said. "I hadn't known about it before and thought it would be a good place to put our items since it was so close to the office."

Silence.

"I'm sorry," he said sweetly. "You have a right to be mad. I meant to tell you this morning but then forgot all about it."

He invited me to lunch. We made peace over a cheeseburger and a soft drink, and then I took the items to Community Bank on First Avenue!

O LORD, SPARE US FROM THESE moments that are starting to affect our marriage! Thank You, however, that what You have brought together not even a senior moment can put asunder!

Grocery Bag Lady

Dear God:

How does my daughter do what she does? Run a house, drive to Little League and music lessons, grocery shop, keep house and volunteer at church. Besides raising kids!

I guess I did the same thing when my children were young, but I sure can't do it all now. I found that out this weekend when I was the stand-in mom while Jennifer and Jack went away for a couple of days.

After playing croquet with Todd, coloring with Mary Ann and overseeing Ted as he made pizza, I was bushed. I looked around and everywhere I glanced there was clutter. I decided to do my daughter and son-in-law a favor and pick up the place before they arrived home.

Then I checked the refrigerator and pantry and saw that they could use a few things. It would be nice for them not to have to run to the market the first thing Monday morning. So I made a list, piled the kids in the van and off we went to the grocery store.

I'm not sure what takes more energy—chasing kids at the park or corralling them at the store and trying to shop at the same time. We made it through the check stand after buying nearly $100 worth of food and got out to the parking lot without losing anyone. I made sure the kids were in the car first. Then I unpacked the grocery bags in the back of the van.

But wouldn't you know it, the kids couldn't keep their hands off one another, so I had to settle a fight between Todd and Ted. Then Mary Ann started crying because Todd took her seat next to the window. That was it. No ice cream stop as I had promised if they cooperated.

I jumped in the driver's seat and darted out of the parking lot fuming under my breath. Suddenly I couldn't wait for Sunday night when their parents would come home and take over.

We pulled into the driveway and I asked each one to pick up one bag and carry it into the house. I popped open the back-door of the van, but there were no bags in sight. The food? Oh no, I realized. It was still in the shopping cart in the middle of the parking lot—unless of course someone took it, a very real possibility.

I was sick! I couldn't bear to start this process all over again, and I sure didn't like the thought of having just lost $100 on food I didn't have. I did the next best thing. I called the store, sure in my mind that it was a lost cause. But once again, dear God, you came through.

The assistant manager answered. "Ma'am we have your bags right here. We put them in storage in the back, assuming some-one would claim them. We'll repack a shopping cart and have it waiting. In fact, if it would be easier, I can have the groceries delivered. Would that help?

Would it? "Absolutely," I said. "You just saved my sanity."

He laughed and by then I could laugh too.

I never did tell my daughter, but I suppose the kids will leak the news that Grandma is at that stage where she is losing her marbles. She can't even grocery shop without having a senior moment.

GOD, I'M SO RELIEVED to know time and again that You are with me even in the mundane circumstances such as grocery shopping. You look after me when I can't seem to look after myself. I love You and thank You.

Good Ol' What's-His-Name!

Dear God:

I'm the queen of senior moments, Lord! I certainly wanted to take back the one I suffered today. I was just so excited about introducing George to my friends at the bridge tournament. Since we were married out of state, most of them couldn't attend the wedding.

Last night I focused on our clothing. I wanted us to knock their socks off. George looks fabulous in blue, so I laid out a light blue shirt, a navy blue vest sweater and blue corduroy slacks. I wore that cute red dress I picked up at Walton's last week.

George was nervous, I could tell. He wanted me to be proud of him, and he hoped my friends would like him. I knew they'd love him. He's a great guy. I'm proud to be on his arm wherever we go.

We arrived at Marion and Bob's house a few minutes late. I hoped by then everyone would be there. We walked into a huge surprise party—with balloons, cake, punch and a banner that read: Congratulations Newlyweds!

I was so shocked and excited that I lost my composure. I looked out at the sea of faces and went absolutely blank!

"Well, aren't you going to introduce us to your handsome groom?" Patsy asked.

"Of course," I said. "Everyone, I'd like you to meet my new husband . . . "

My voice faded to a whisper and stopped cold! There was a long moment of self-conscious silence as everyone waited for me to furnish a name. God, You're my witness. You heard me. Wasn't that awful? I turned to George as though I had never met the man before!

"Oh dear," I muttered to my bewildered husband, "what *is* your name?"

Not exactly the best way to start one's marriage. Then suddenly it was there on the tip of my tongue. "*George!*" I blurted out. Thank You, God!

I FELT LIKE MELTING into the floor, O Lord. But You held me up as You do in all situations. Thank You that You know me by name and my husband too. You never forget. What would I do without You during these confounding senior moments?

Who's on First?

Dear God:

Five women over 55! Get a group like this together and you're sure to have a few senior moments. My friends and I sat around a large table in Betty's home, chatting and enjoying a delicious potluck salad lunch—our first get-together following summer vacations.

Some women sat in armchairs, others in chairs without arms. Lois sat in an armless chair, and Sharon was seated next to her in an armchair. All was well until we finished dessert and began taking turns sharing our various travels and other adventures.

Sharon excused herself for a doctor's appointment while the rest of us refilled our glasses with iced tea. Back at the table, Lois suddenly wanted to change seats. After listening to the conversation that followed, I was ready for a nap.

"Hmm, that armchair looks a lot more comfortable than this chair," Lois lamented, pointing to the one Sharon had been sitting in before she left.

"Go ahead and move over," Alice directed.

"But someone is sitting there," responded Lois.

"Not at the moment!" Nancy piped up.

I noticed Lois blushing. True. The seat was empty—but it had been occupied by "What's-Her-Name"!

"But, but someone," she struggled to come up with the name, "was sitting there," she said, defending herself in this moment of forgetfulness. "She . . . she . . . might come back."

"Sharon. That was Sharon's seat," Alice shot back, perhaps annoyed that Lois couldn't remember Sharon's name.

"Oh!" exclaimed Lois.

A touchy moment turned to laughter, as we all admitted any one of us could have made the same mistake. Sharon did not return, so the armchair went to Lois—or was that Alice or Nancy?

Next time I think we'll just meet at the park and sit on the grass!

OH, DEAR GOD, whether or not we find the right chair for us here on Earth matters little as long as we keep in mind that You have established a place for each one of us in heaven.

Back Burner

Dear God:

I'm famous for putting things on the back burner—like paying bills, organizing my desk, filing paperwork, balancing my checkbook. Yesterday I found out how true this is! I decided to cook dinner for Donna and me. After 40 years of marriage, I figured it was my turn to put a meal on the table. I was quite proud of myself for coordinating the items on my list. I put a pot of vegetables on the back burner to steam, while I sautéed fish on the front burner. Rolls were in the oven, and a fruit salad was chilling in the fridge.

When all was ready, I called my wife to dinner. We dished up our portions and then sat down to eat. A strained expression crossed her face.

"What's going on?" I asked.

"Honey, I think the broccoli needs a little more time."

"What do you mean?" I barked. "I timed this meal perfectly."

"Maybe it's just me," she said. "They're too crisp for my taste. But the fish is delicious," she said, trying to win me back. "It's nice and tender—and hot," she said. "What happened to the veggies?"

"What do you mean, 'what happened'?" I asked. "Nothing happened. I've been out here cooking for the last 30 minutes. Looks good to me. Dig in."

"That's just it," Donna said. "I'd have to dig to eat the broccoli! I'm wondering if you put the pot on the broken burner," she added.

"Of course not," I said, defending myself. "I turned on the right burner. Look for yourself. It's still warm. Put your hand over it."

Donna admitted I was right. The coil on the right back burner was red, but I had set the pot on the left back burner and that coil was black!

I was caught red-handed, so to speak. We put the fish in the fridge and headed out the door laughing. We went to a local café and enjoyed a complete meal, prepared on a stove that works!

THANK YOU, GOD, that when we're "cooking" with You, we never have to worry about defending ourselves. Your ways are good and true and they always work.

Nailed!

Dear God:

Life in our house is like a game of Hide-and-Seek. My husband hides (misplaces is more like it) everything from his name badge needed for work to his car keys to his favorite cap—and even his glasses.

When he began mumbling one day as he walked from room to room, I didn't think much of it—assuming he was on the hunt for something he'd lost. I carried on watering and fertilizing our plants. I'm learning to back off—especially now that I have high blood pressure! Later I heard him laughing in another room. I went to find out what was so funny.

He had been looking for the nails he was sure he had set down somewhere as he looked for his missing hammer while working on a project in the laundry room. The hammer showed up on the kitchen counter. The nails, well, were hanging from his mouth. He had put them there when he needed two hands to carry in a piece of wood.

That afternoon I went shopping, mumbling to myself about the state of affairs in our home. Dan couldn't keep track of his hammer and nails, and I couldn't keep track of Dan and his annoying penchant for losing things.

I decided to "fix" Dan and take care of my blood pressure at the same time. I bought him a tool apron for his birthday, one with a special slot for a hammer and a small pouch in front for nails. Then I returned home and handed him his gift—six months early! I didn't have the patience to wait till his real birthday.

IT'S GOOD TO KNOW that when we find You, O Lord, our search is over. You are all we ever need.

*S*hould 'a Stayed in Bed!

Dear God:

What is going on with me? Yesterday was a day to end all days. I was about to turn on the television to watch the evening news when suddenly the phone rang. I picked up the receiver. "Hello, this is Margaret," I said. No one responded and the phone rang again.

Of course! I was holding the TV remote control. Next thing you know I'll be trying to watch television by using the telephone receiver!

Next I went into the bathroom to brush my teeth before bed. I picked up my toothbrush and proceeded to brush my hair. At that rate, it would certainly take a long time to do the 100 strokes my mother required of me when I was a child.

Then I reached into the medicine cabinet to get the asthma medication for my cat. I took the pills out of the bottle and then absentmindedly popped them into my mouth and swallowed them before I realized what I had done.

I wasn't sure whether to call the vet for my cat or a psychiatrist for me. I called the pharmacy instead. I was relieved to learn that the same asthma medication works for cats and humans, so it wouldn't do me any harm.

I decided I'd had enough senior moments for one day, so I climbed into bed and purred myself to sleep!

THANK YOU, LORD, that in Your Word You promise that when we lie down our sleep will be sweet. After a day like yesterday, I was happy to take You up on that wonderful promise.

Truckin' with Hubby

Dear God:

When Dick invited me to join him on one of his long hauls, I said yes. It sounded like an adventure and I was ready for something new. It would be fun to be together on the open highway, cruisin' along like the two TV characters who used to drive from one state to another on Route 66.

Reality wasn't exactly that glamorous, but we did have fun, and at our age I'm more game than ever for a bit of fun. I started each day reading a couple of devotions while Dick drove. Then I checked e-mail as we bounced down the highway through Nevada and Utah. We stopped for the night at the Flying J in Richfield, Utah. We found a cute western café where we had dinner and then breakfast the next day. We took advantage of the private coed shower (whoo! whoo!) available there and at many places along the way.

On Sunday one of our tires went flat! There was no chance of getting it repaired that day, so we limped up the road through the Rockies, checking the tire every so often and hoping we'd make it to the next stop. We finally reached the warehouse, our destination, at 11:00 P.M., where we were to unload Monday morning. We slept well that night!

The next morning, I learned how to thump tires and climb in and out of the cab 100 times a day. I even helped with directions, which will surprise most of my friends since, as You know, Lord, I do not have the gift of navigation!

We reached Santa Fe about dinnertime. "Do you think we can find the Blue Corn Café?" Dick asked.

"It's somewhere near a main intersection," I said, stifling a laugh. Lots of help I was. "Lord," I prayed, "You know we'd like to go to the Blue Corn Café, but if it's not close by, please help us find good Mexican food somewhere."

I opened my eyes, looked up and there was the Blue Corn Café right in front of us! We walked in, plopped down in a comfy booth and enjoyed a delicious meal.

That night I couldn't stop thinking of how gracious You are, dear Lord. You showed us throughout the trip that You are as concerned about the little things in our lives as much as the big things.

As I look back now, I realize how special it was for these two seniors, Dick and I, to spend this time together on the open road, under the stars and even under the cab of his truck. Whatever we did, we did it together. I now have a greater under-standing and appreciation for why my husband loves the open road so much and the excitement of truckin' down the highway.

Would I go again someday? You bet.

LORD, I THANK YOU for the unexpected pleasures and surpris-es that each new day brings. May I always keep You as the focal point of my daily affairs and watch as You unfold one blessing after another.

The Visitor

Dear God:

I have always prided myself on being a genteel Southern lady, soft-spoken and with mannerisms that showed good breeding. I think of myself as polite, conversant and willing to help when called upon.

People tell me that I'm a compassionate person who cares about those less fortunate than I am. And many look at me and say I'm "well-preserved" for my age (78 and counting!) thanks to a selective diet, daily walks, afternoon naps and a life free of financial stress.

Why, Lord, I've never felt so good as I do these days. I am determined to stay this way and to living out my final years in the home Clem and I built in 1951.

But sometimes, dear God, I wonder if it's worth all this effort to stay alive and well. So many of my friends have gone, and now I'm a widow too. If I want to see the few women friends I have left, I have to go to their nursing homes or retirement facilities. I don't mind *visiting* these places, but I wouldn't want to *live* in one.

Imagine, Lord, what a surprise I got when I visited Grace last week at Twin Valley Nursing Home. I plopped on the extra bed in her room—to relax while we talked. Since she didn't have a roommate, I didn't see the harm in it.

But I wasn't there 10 minutes when someone tried to trap me into staying. Remember when the nurse's aid walked in with a lunch tray, set it down in front of Grace, then backed out with a huge apology?

"I'm so sorry, ma'am," she said looking me straight in the eye. "I'm new on the floor. I didn't know you had moved in. I'll get your lunch right away."

That did it, Lord. I snatched up my purse from the chair beside the bed, and hurried out the door, waving good-bye to Grace as I flew down the hallway. "I'm just a *visitor*!" I shouted. "I don't live here!"

As I write about this, I'm laughing out loud. Whew! What a narrow escape. I think I'll visit with Grace on the phone from now on.

LORD, I HOPE I never have to live in a nursing home. I'd rather be a visitor. Wherever I live, though, I guess I am a visitor—till You call me home to heaven. That's something to look forward to.

Left Behind

Dear God:

Today at work I had the scare of my life! I was busy at my computer, sipping coffee and listening to some soft music. I felt relaxed and happy after a long and difficult meeting earlier in the day.

Suddenly Mr. Lockhart walked from one cubicle to the next. As he spoke to the various employees, each one gathered a jacket or purse or briefcase and walked out of the office. I work in the corner, so I couldn't tell what was happening. I assumed he was calling a special meeting; if he needed me he'd stop by. Meanwhile, I got up and went to the ladies' room.

When I returned I was the only soul in the place. The first thing I thought of was the rapture. Jesus had come back and I had been left behind! I grabbed hold of the first desk I passed and shouted, "Help! Where is everyone?"

Suddenly Mr. Lockhart appeared, surprised that I had not heard him the first time. I explained that I had been in the restroom.

"There's been a bomb threat," he said in a deliberate voice. "Gather your things and leave the building. You won't be coming back today."

I WAS RELIEVED TO KNOW YOU HAD NOT forgotten me, Lord. If You do come back soon, and You don't see me right away, please check the ladies' room. I spend a lot of time there these days!

Hardening of the Nails

Dear God:

I wish You had given me strong fingernails—like Ella's. She doesn't pay any attention to hers except for an occasional plain manicure, yet they always look nice. Not mine. If I don't take care of them regularly, they break and split, even more so now that I'm older.

I've spent a lot of money on those nail-hardening products, but they don't seem to do any good. I keep using them, though, hoping my nails will eventually become stronger.

Last night before bed, I decided to put on another coat and let it dry while watching the late news. What an ordeal that turned out to be. I spent 20 minutes on a task that should take about 60 seconds.

The liquid is clear, so it doesn't matter if I don't do a perfect job. I polished the nails on my right hand and then got absorbed in a news item about an abduction in my town. When I returned to my nails, I couldn't remember for the life of me if I had done the left hand too. Both were dry and shiny. I had not removed the first coat from last week.

To be on the safe side, I polished the nails on my left hand, then trotted out to the kitchen for a glass of water. I noticed a plant on the counter was starting to droop, so I shared my water with the little fella and then walked back to the den. I saw the polish and then realized I was confused about what I had or had not done.

Finally, I shut off the television and got down to business with no distractions. I polished the nails on both hands—again—and then went to bed! I realized this morning that a good night's rest is more important than hard nails.

GOD, CAN YOU BELIEVE THE THINGS I get myself into? I'm just too interested in what's going on around me. Please help me to focus on one task at a time—prayer being at the top of my list!

Part 3:
Embarrassing
Moments

$\mathcal{G}$one with the Wind

Dear God:

I'm reminded today of that humiliating moment in January 2000, when I was at the Super Bowl in Atlanta. It should have been a proud moment for me, since Allison, my daughter, was performing in the halftime show. But instead it was a stupid, shameful moment. It was more of a Stupid Bowl than a Super Bowl!

I'll never forget halftime when volunteers were allowed to sit on the Tennessee Titans' bench to watch the show. Several from our group—which included college students and a few middle-aged and senior adults—thought it might be fun to "lift" a Gatorade towel as a souvenir.

Looking back, this may have been a typical college prank, but it was not typical for an aging Christian woman. I don't know what caused this temporary lapse of sanity, though I'm having more and more these days!

My timing was extremely bad. The security people were decidedly fed up with fans helping themselves to souvenirs. They caught me, red-handed, clutching the stolen goods as I was leaving the field. I didn't get too far. In fact, you might say I had to throw in the towel. I handed it to a big, burly guy who stared down at me as if I were two-feet tall.

"Just how *old* are you, lady?" he asked.

"Too old—and old enough to know better," I responded meekly.

"Burly" was clearly disgusted with me. He told one of the guards to arrest me. I sobbed on the spot, but it didn't matter. I was the scapegoat and that was that!

"Please," I pleaded. "I lost my mind for a moment. I'm so sorry. I'll never do anything like this again."

Too late! It was off to the Georgia Dome dungeon for me. Perhaps even off with my head!

But then you came in like a merciful gust of wind, O God. A rush of cold air blasted into the Dome wind tunnel, threatening to blow apart some very expensive 20-foot tall Disney puppets. The security guard left me to chase them down, and he never came back. I did not go looking for him either, though it took days for me to let go of the notion that he'd be back sometime when I least expected. By that time I was beyond remorse and repentance. I felt ashamed, upset, ugly, stupid and guilty!

Yes, it was wrong to "lift" the towel, and I will never do it again, I promise—whether at the Super Bowl or the Super 8 Motel.

WHEW! THANKS TO YOU, O LORD, my sin has "gone with the wind." Now I know in a deep and personal way the truth of Psalm 25:8-9: "The Lord is good and glad to teach the proper path to all who go astray; he will teach the ways that are right and best to those who humbly turn to him" (*TLB*).

Midnight Alarm!

Dear God:

What a trip this has been. I just have to write to You about it, even though You already know what happened! Hubby and I had been traveling around the southwestern corner of Australia in our Caravan (recreational van), when we decided to stop overnight at the home of my husband's cousin, Harry.

We were just getting settled for the night when suddenly a loud knock on the bedroom door awakened us at about 1:00 A.M. Harry told us that our car alarm was going off and he feared someone was breaking into the vehicle.

Paul hopped out of bed and went to have a look. After going around the car several times, checking doors and windows, he realized it was not our car making the noise but rather an alarm on a house across the road.

Paul came back in the house and stopped to tell his cousin what happened. Then he went back to bed.

The following morning, Paul awakened, looked at me and said, "I don't even have a car alarm," and then scratched his head and broke out laughing. At that point, I wondered whether the event really occurred or whether he was simply sleepwalking in the night! Seniors are known to do such things, aren't they Lord?

HOW FUNNY WE ARE AS WE AGE. Such unthinkable things happen and we become obsessed with them. It's simply "not like me," we muse, only to realize it really is like us—for we are seniors after all! I'm so grateful You are with us through it all and that what we do never embarrasses You.

Heads Up!

Dear God:

Finally, my husband and I agreed that we needed an electric blanket. Since we have different needs (I'm cold and George is always hot), we decided that a dual-controlled, digital readout electric blanket was the perfect solution. We each could set our preferred temperature.

We unpacked it and put it on our bed. I couldn't wait to try it out. That night, I crawled into bed and turned it on. Darn! One side worked (my husband's) but mine did not. Disappointed, we returned it to the store. George thought we should try another manufacturer. But neither of us wanted to do the footwork, so we settled for another blanket from the same company. We drove home, put the new blanket on the bed and turned up the controls on both sides to High (H).

When I got in on my side, it was too hot, so I tried turning the control down to 3 or 4. Something was clearly wrong! I couldn't get it to go below 7.

Was I mad! We had traveled over 400 miles (in the two trips) and still didn't have a functional blanket.

The next day we drove back to the store. By this time, the sales clerk looked at us as if we were loony. "Why are you returning the second blanket?" she asked.

"Because the control will not go below 7," I said, feeling indignant. "I can't sleep with that much heat." I carried on about the poor quality of the manufacturer of this blanket that had been so highly recommended to us.

Patiently, the young woman took the control panel and turned it upside down and showed me that I what I had seen as a number 7 was actually the letter L (for Low). My face must have been apple red at that point.

The blanket was fine. It was my mind that was messed up! George and I scurried out the door as I hung my head and whispered a silent prayer of thanks.

THANK YOU, God, for allowing me to laugh at myself! And for Your assurance that no matter how much of a pickle I get myself into, You'll always be there to calm me down and show me a solution.

Paper Trail

Dear God:

I was so excited that morning. It was finally the day of the charity luncheon I'd been talking about for months. I was one of the hostesses, and I wanted to look and feel beautiful! I rushed into the hotel just before noon when the festivities were about to begin, trotted down the hallway, turned right and popped into the ladies' room.

You know what happened next! Another of those "moments" that are beginning to take over my life occurred. I freshened my lipstick and brushed lint from my suit. *It's now or never*, I thought, as I stepped into the hallway. If they don't like me the way I am, well, it's too late now.

I was feeling great, Lord, when suddenly a young man ran up beside me and gently pulled me aside.

"Excuse me, ma'am, but . . . well, I don't know how to say this, but . . . well, there seems to be some paper attached to your . . . your skirt. You might want to check it out."

How impudent, I thought. "What are you talking about?" I asked.

The young hotel employee hurried off and I stood there feeling abandoned. I glanced at my reflection in a shop window and nearly fainted. Mortified, I turned and ran back to the ladies' room to sever the paper that had caught in my panty hose and trailed behind me like a bridal train!

WHAT NEXT, LORD? I can see that I need to slow down, stop, look and listen to You before I rush into things unprepared. Thank You for the reminder to be still and know that You are God, and to remember that You are *for* me even when I embarrass myself.

$\mathcal{B}$rrrr!

Dear God:

I'm laughing about a past mistake on this warm and sunny day as I throw open the window for a breath of fresh air. Remember, just months ago, when the temperatures fell and I was shivering in my little office?

One day I walked into the room, turned on the computer, pulled out the keyboard and massaged my cold fingers. Before sitting down, I dragged out the small electric space heater from the storage closet and plugged the cord into the wall socket. *Ah,* I thought, *warm air will soon flow.* I'd be calm and cozy enough to complete the project I'd been working on for several days.

I plopped down on my chair and bowed my head to offer you this day and all the work I planned to do. But my fingers felt like ice cubes. I could barely type a full sentence they were so stiff. I stopped several times to rub my hands together and wiggle my toes that were just as cold.

I glanced at the heater. The coils were gray. *That's odd,* I thought. Generally they're red when they're functioning properly. Again and again I stopped to massage my freezing fingers and toes, feeling a bit impatient now. *What's going on?* I wondered. I hope I don't need to repair this old heater, or worse, replace it. Maybe it's just worn out!

I bent down to check the on-off knob. It was in the off position. *Hello! It helps to turn on the heater,* I told myself. And that's just what I did.

Today I can laugh at this silly mistake, God, and even be thankful for living alone—where no one is around to witness such senior moments.

OF COURSE YOU SEE ALL THINGS, GOD, and I am grateful for that. You provide the grace and wisdom and common sense I need when I'm fresh out! Thank You for caring—even when the biggest problem of the day is simply remembering to turn on my space heater *and* my mind!

Burner Buddies

Dear God:

What is with me? I'm doing at 60 years of age what I did at 20—and I'm not talking about running a marathon or climbing a mountain. I'm doing dumb stuff like burning pots and pans, and steaming vegetables till they turn to soup (without intending to).

I remember the day I put water on to boil in a cheap aluminum pan, then ran out to check the mail. I saw my neighbor in her garden so I stopped by to chat. I never thought of the water again—that is until I walked back into the house and the smell of burning metal hit my nostrils!

"Oh no!" I shrieked. The water had not only boiled away, but the pan had bonded itself to the electric burner! I had to pay the landlord to replace the stove.

The memory of that costly mistake still haunts me 30-some years later. But I learned my lesson. Now I set a kitchen timer when I'm cooking and carry it around with me till it goes off! I don't dare set it down somewhere and leave the room, though, because I can't trust my ears to hear it. Oh the joy of getting older!

GOD, YOU PROMISE TO BE WITH US in the ups and downs of life, so I'm not going to worry about setting the house on fire. I'm going to focus, instead, on listening to Your voice, because You promise to guide me in everything I think, say and do.

$\mathscr{A}$ Good Time

Dear God:

Yesterday while having lunch at a local restaurant, I overheard two older men talking with one another. They exchanged stories about their golf and bridge games, and their escalating health problems—one with a hearing loss, Ben, and the other with a bum knee, Earl.

I thought they were probably old friends, but as the conversation progressed, I wasn't so sure. Then they hauled out some photos of their families, including grandchildren and even a great-grandchild or two. They seemed bent on outdoing one another, especially Ben, the one with the hearing problem. His voice reached shouting volume. I know this can happen with people who don't hear so well. Pretty soon heads were turning in their direction. I heard a few customers yell, "Shush!"

About that time, Earl, the man with the bum knee, pointed to a picture of his wife. With a catch in his throat, he told Ben that she had gone to heaven the month before.

"Oh, that's nice," Ben responded. "I hope she has a good time!"

Earl was speechless.

GOOD LORD, CAN YOU IMAGINE? We do say the darnedest things when we don't know or can't hear what's going on. Fortunately, when we reach that stage, we can turn to You and know You will make all things work together for good, even those embarrassing moments.

$\mathcal{P}$erfect Coiffure

Dear God:

As You know I've been trying for years to settle on the ideal hairstyle—one that fits my face and my stage in life, especially now that I'm an octogenarian.

Last week I finally settled on something I can live with. I made an appointment with a hairdresser and my daughter agreed to drive me to her shop.

"Do you know what look you want?" the stylist asked.

I assured her I knew. With that we proceeded to the shampoo bowl. I felt a tingle of excitement as she turned on the water and began to wash my hair with a silvery mixture that would bring out the highlights. It was only a matter of minutes before I'd look smashing again.

Then it happened. As we returned to her booth, the woman paused, comb and scissors in hand, eager to perform her magic. "Okay," she said, "I'm ready. What style do you want?"

I sat there, my face growing warmer by the moment as a trickle of water slid down my neck. I couldn't, for the life of me, remember what I wanted!

"Whatever you think will look good on me," I fibbed. "You're the expert."

I couldn't bear to admit my senior moment!

O GOD, I CAN RELATE TO THAT EXPERIENCE. How often I set my mind on a movie I want to see, a book I'm dying to read, a recipe I'm eager to prepare, but when it comes right down to the "doing," I can't remember what it was. What a blessing it is for me that I can turn to You and whisper my dilemma. You've never failed me yet! Thank You for that.

Right There, All Right!

Dear God:

Miriam and I went shopping today for groceries and vita-mins. I like going with her. What I forget she remembers, and what she forgets I seem to remember. We're a perfect duet!

We had fun gathering what we needed and stopping for a cup of tea on the way home. We always have so much to talk about.

After our outing, we said good-bye and promised to get together again next week. She went her way and I went mine. But when I got home, I realized I didn't have the bottle of vitamins I had been so intent on purchasing. *Nuts*, I thought. *Now I'll have to make another trip and I have so much to do already.* How careless of me.

But then it occurred to me that my bottle might have gone into Miriam's bag by accident. It couldn't hurt to check and might even save me a return trip.

I phoned Miriam and she looked through her things, but my vitamins weren't there. She dashed over to help me find them. We both knew I had paid for the bottle at the check stand.

Then came the moment of reckoning! I opened the cabinet where I usually keep my vitamins and voilà, there stood the bot-tle in plain view—right where it belonged. Oh dear! I surely need whatever is in each of those little tablets that calms the nerves and stimulates the brain!

WHAT DO YOU MAKE OF THIS, O GOD? Now it appears I need to have my eyesight checked. It's surely time for a new pair of glasses—ones that will help me see clearly what is right in front of my nose! And bring on the raw carrots too!

$\mathcal{H}$iding Place

Dear God:

It's always nice to catch someone else having a senior moment. Heaven knows others catch me often enough. Today I was quite annoyed with my husband. I had just used a fresh tea towel in the kitchen, but when I went to reach for it a second time, I couldn't find it anywhere. I asked my husband where it was. Only a moment before, I had seen him using it to wipe a cup. He didn't know what he had done with it either, so together we searched the kitchen and then the adjoining rooms.

This is ridiculous, I thought. *Where could such an item disappear to when there are only the two of us in the same room at the same time?*

I was thoroughly frustrated by the time we finished looking. No tea towel in sight. I took out a clean one and sat down with my cup. My husband carried on with what he was doing.

A moment later, he opened the refrigerator to pour himself a glass of juice. Just then I heard a muffled giggle. I jumped up to see what it was about. There, to his surprise and mine, was the missing tea towel, rolled into a tiny ball and tucked away in the corner of the top shelf!

O LORD, THAT ONE IS A BIT TOO CLOSE FOR COMFORT. How many times have I done something similar, like the time I put the phone in the drawer and tried to hang up the hairbrush, or discovered a bottle of hair gel in the refrigerator and a bottle of salad dressing in the bathroom cabinet? That's what I get for being distracted so easily. Teach me to focus on You, first of all, and then on what's in front of me to do in that moment.

Cell-itis

Dear God:

Today, Claire called, but I could hardly concentrate on what she was saying because I had misplaced my cell phone and I needed it for some urgent business.

Apparently, Claire could hear the commotion as I tried to listen to her and do a thorough search of my purse at the same time. Finally, she interrupted me. "What is going on, Martha? We seem to have a scratchy connection. There is a lot of noise at your end."

"I'm sorry," I told her and stopped the search immediately. "I don't mean to be rude. It's just that I seem to have lost my cell phone and I'm panicking."

"Martha," she said, stifling a giggle, "it's in your hand. You're talking to me on it."

Enough said. I ended the conversation quickly and promptly sat down and had a good laugh—and then a good cry!

SEE WHAT I MEAN, LORD? Just when I think I have it together, it all comes apart. But You're here for me and that's all that matters. Good thing You take my calls day or night and no phone is needed.

Anyone for Tea?

Dear God:

As I put on the coffee this morning, I double-checked the pot and the water holder. It's become a habit ever since Mom experienced a most embarrassing moment when she made a fresh pot using an electric percolator.

She served her guests and then noticed strange looks wash across their faces. She was suddenly nervous, wondering if she had used too much coffee, making it too strong. Or maybe the eggshells she used to purify the coffee had gone bad somehow.

When the guests left, Mom collected their half-full cups and poured the remaining liquid down the drain. Then she emptied the pot and was horrified to find the cause of the bad coffee!

A dead mouse—out cold at the bottom of the pot!

How did she ever get over such an incident, dear God? With laughter and humility, I guess, though her friends were no help! One in particular enjoyed reminding her of the incident whenever they got together.

"Don't put Edith in charge of coffee," she chanted.

I believe it was then that Mom switched to tea! Today she knows how to handle every embarrassing moment. Bring them to You, Lord, and leave them there.

DEAR LORD, I HOPE I WILL follow that example when such moments occur in my life. You help us to take life in stride, leaving the crises and the results in Your hands where they truly belong.

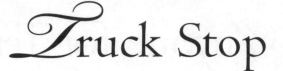Truck Stop

Dear God:

Cars and trucks are great—when they work. But when they break down or make annoying noises that I cannot find, well then, I wonder if I wouldn't be better off walking!

Last week was the last straw with my truck. For several days, I heard a sloshing sound every time I accelerated. At first, I didn't think much of it. I had just gotten my oil changed and my tires rotated. The mechanic told me everything was in top shape.

Easy for him to say. He doesn't have to drive my vehicle. I put up with this nuisance for another few days. Finally, one day, I got fed up. I hit my limit. I was ready to go into the shop and punch someone in the nose. I had paid good money for the checkup, and here I was unsatisfied with the work. Going into the shop again meant more time and more money—two items I am continually short of, as you might know.

I called Bob's Auto and asked to speak with Bob himself. I was not going to fool around with the underlings! It was time to get this problem straightened out once and for all.

"How can I help you?" Bob asked patiently. Apparently, he had dealt with a few other hysterical females before.

I told him about the sloshing sound and asked if he would take a look if I brought in my truck right away. I didn't want to deal with one of his incompetent mechanics.

"Sure, Ms. Winkler, bring it right in."

I dropped everything and headed for Bob's Auto, eager to find out what the real problem was and also to see Bob light into the mechanic who had done the work originally.

I sat in the waiting room—waiting! A few moments later, Bob appeared in the doorway with a smile—make that a smirk—on his face.

"Ms. Winkler, I believe I've located the problem," he said, stifling a laugh. Then he pulled a half-gallon container of drinking water from behind his back and presented it to me. It had slid underneath the driver's seat.

"No charge," he said. "It's been our pleasure to do business with you."

I was too embarrassed to laugh, but I managed to smile with my eyes glued to the floor.

"Uh, thanks," I muttered. "I'm sorry for the trouble I caused."

LORD, I'M STRUCK BY THE TROUBLE I've caused You by my arrogance and self-righteousness. Help me to learn from this humorous and humiliating experience.

The Perfect Pair

Dear God:

Here's one for the books! My friend Claudia and I carefully planned our trip to Atlanta in June for a book convention. We spent time on the phone comparing notes—talking about what clothing to bring and accessories to choose, and about the kind of shoes that would be most comfortable for walking around the convention floor two days in a row.

Finally, we settled on our wardrobes, checked and double-checked our plane tickets, and made sure we had enough spending money for food and extras.

The day we arrived at the convention it was pouring rain. Since we don't think much about rain in California, Claudia and I never thought to bring a raincoat. I had a small umbrella, so we walked pretty close together to stay under it at the same time. Quite a sight since she's tall and I'm short! We had some good laughs about all our planning only to discover that the one thing we really needed—rain gear—was not on either of our lists.

But that's not all. By the third day, we were loopy with fatigue, aching feet and an overdose of excitement. That evening before rushing off to one of the banquets, Claudia took an extra moment or two to decide what to wear. That meant choosing the appropriate pair of shoes, as well. She reached into the closet, pulled out two shoes and asked my opinion.

"Should I wear the light beige pair?" she asked, holding up one for me to see. "Or would the tan be better with my dress?"

She pulled out a second shoe and held it up for me to examine.

"I can't tell the difference," I said, squinting. "In fact, I'm wondering why you brought two pairs of shoes that look so much alike," I said. "It seems either of these would work."

She stepped into the light with one shoe in each hand. Then she burst out laughing. They were the same. She was holding the left shoe in one hand and its mate in the other!

"If the shoes fit, and they match," I joked, "I'd say wear them!"

She slipped into her dress, donned the shoes and off we went, laughing all the way to the elevator.

GOD, I'M GLAD I HAVE FRIENDS to go through this stage of life with me. I don't feel so alone! But then I should never feel alone. You're always with me. You've promised to never leave me nor forsake me—even when I have an embarrassing moment.

*T*rick or Treat

Dear God:

It's getting complicated even to go out for lunch with a friend. Yesterday Gloria and I met at El Pollo Loco. I love the place—plenty of fresh salad makings, broiled chicken, a nice selection of beverages and discounts for seniors. Gloria and I qualify, as you know.

Earlier that day, however, I had received some disturbing news. My sister, Jane, from Arizona had suffered a stroke. I felt shaken and was easily distracted after that. Still, I didn't want to break my date with Gloria. In fact, I reasoned it would be good to talk about the incident with a caring friend.

Gloria arrived in a flurry, because she was late getting away from her job and knew I had been waiting awhile. When we reached the front of the line, Gloria insisted I go first. I gave my order along with a coupon I had saved. The cashier studied it to see if it was valid. Then I asked if the senior discount also applied. She gave me the cup for my beverage and went to check on the discount. When she returned with a negative response, I thanked her for checking, picked up my cup and headed for a table. Then I went back to the cashier to tell Gloria where I was seated. She was fumbling with her money to pay for my lunch since I'd walked off without paying! How embarrassing.

After more fumbling, I provided the few cents needed to complete the transaction. Gloria insisted on treating me at that point since she'd already handed the cashier the necessary dollar bills.

As we turned to leave, the patient, long-suffering cashier spoke up. "Ma'am," she said to Gloria, "did you want to order a lunch for yourself?"

Well, of course she did! But being seniors, apparently we were incapable of ordering two meals at once, each paying for our own and actually eating without being fed!

We certainly had a good chuckle over the whole affair as we finally enjoyed our lunch. We're in our early 60s now, so can you imagine, God, what we'll be like when we reach 70?

GOD, IT'S GOOD THAT YOU CAN LAUGH with us instead of at us! I like remembering that being merry is the perfect antidote for almost any situation.

A Good Nap

Dear God:

I have to write about this even though you already know what happened. But you're so good that way. You let me tell my stories over and over, unlike some people I know!

Chloris, a friend who lives here in our retirement community, was working part-time in Richmond, Virginia, this past winter. She would drive from Newport News, Rhode Island, to Richmond each Tuesday morning and return the following Friday afternoon. That seems like quite a haul to me. And apparently it was for her too, based on what she told me happened to her one Monday afternoon. Fatigue caught up with her that day as she was out and about doing some errands.

She began feeling drowsy about 4 P.M., so she went home and took a short nap before dinner was to be served at 6 P.M. She overslept, however, and didn't awaken until 7:30 P.M. She glanced at the clock and assumed it was Tuesday morning, so she dressed, picked up her overnight bag and headed for her car. When she reached the lobby of our facility, someone asked, "Where are you going?"

It was clear she was not heading for the dining room.

"I'm going to work," Chloris responded cheerfully, "but it seems unusually dark for 7:30 in the morning, doesn't it?"

She heard a couple of people chuckle and then one spoke up and set her straight.

"It's 7:30 P.M. on Monday night," the woman said.

Chloris told me later that she turned promptly, took the elevator back to her apartment, undressed and set her alarm clock for 7:30 A.M.

LORD, I WANT TO LIVE IN "KINGDOM" TIME, on Your timetable, by Your clock. Then I will always be in sync with what *You* have for me—whether sleeping or awake.

$\mathscr{S}$ay That Again!

Dear God:

What did You think of me at that wedding a few days ago? It was the first time I had seen some of those people in years. I remember the two women I chatted with at the reception. It was fun to recall old times, especially since I had taught their children in school.

I was proud of myself for remembering the name of one of them—Maureen Kelly. It came quite easily, actually. The other lady's name I simply could not recall no matter how hard I tried. And I couldn't remember the names of their sons, even though they had been in my class.

The following Wednesday night I saw the "woman without a name" in choir just two rows in front of me. I leaned over to a friend seated next to me and asked, "What is Inez Vaughn's name?"

My friend jumped and looked at me. "What?" she asked incredulously.

"Never mind," I said, as I shrank down in my seat. "I didn't say anything, okay?"

GOD, IT'S A GOOD THING You have more than one name: Almighty, Creator, King, Savior, Lord and so many others. There's no chance I'll forget Your name, and I know that You will never forget my name—or me—even into eternity. How comforting to know that.

Clothes Encounter

Dear God:

How difficult can it be? I mean, I thought I had it all figured out, planned even, so I wouldn't have to think before washing clothes or stashing the trash.

Keep it simple, I told myself, when I set up the laundry area in our new home.

Washing machine. Check.

Dryer. Check.

Clothes hamper. Check.

Trash compactor. Check.

Shelf for cleaning products, laundry soap, rags. Check. Check. Check!

What could be more straightforward? I'm not sure, but apparently I need more training. That's twice now—in one day—that I've tossed my dirty clothes into the trash compactor and the trash into the clothes hamper. If I keep this up, I'll have the cleanest leftovers in town and a wardrobe fit for a Barbie doll.

God, these senior moments are getting to me, as You can see. I remember the proverb that says my days will be many and You will add years to my life (see Prov. 9:11). Assuming that's true, I'm going to need some new clothes—and fast! Make them extra, extra large, in case I can't break this habit with the compactor.

LORD, YOU ARE SO GOOD TO ME. You shore me up even when I embarrass myself, when I'm alone and have no one to laugh with about such things. You are here with me, holding me close and reminding me that nothing can separate me from Your love and acceptance. What a relief it is to know that. And what fun it is to talk to You about these crazy moments.

$\mathscr{S}$omething's Fishy!

Dear God:

You know how Mel and I love to fish. Yesterday we motored out to our favorite spot. I took a deep breath and relaxed. We had a whole day to ourselves. I packed a picnic lunch, loaded the cooler with cold drinks and plenty of water, and I even remembered to bring our his-and-hers matching fishing jackets! Mel won me over shortly after we were married. I *now* enjoy fishing as much as he does. And I can tell a lure from a line! How about that?

The shoreline was covered with greenery, a pretty contrast to the blue, blue sky. Thank You for making this perfect setting and for giving us such a beautiful day to be out in Your creation.

We motored out to what we thought would be an ideal spot. The fish appeared to be biting; we were ready for them. We decided to drop the anchor since we were planning to be there for a good, long time. Mel dropped it and I watched as he fed the rope out. When the last coil plopped over, I noticed that we continued to drift. Something was clearly wrong.

Then we both remembered at the same time! We forgot to tie the anchor rope to the boat.

Oh, these senior moments! What's to become of us now that we're having them at the same time in the same situation? Help, Lord!

When You went fishing with Your friends, dear God, I bet You didn't forget anything as important as tying the rope to the boat. But even if You did, You could correct it immediately!

I TRUST YOU TO DO THE SAME FOR ME. May I see You as my true anchor in all situations whether large or small.

$\mathcal{F}$lat Tired!

Dear God:

Here I am proud to have lived this long, still able to work, care for my home and fix most things that break or leak. Until today, I was also proud that I could change a tire when most of my friends wouldn't even consider it.

I was in one big hurry this morning, as You know, afraid of being late for work (that alarm really does need replacing), and then I was greeted with a flat tire.

I called the office and told Roberta I'd be late due to the flat tire. She suggested I call my auto service, but I didn't want to wait that long. I knew I could change the tire before the tow truck would arrive. *You can do this,* I told myself. *You've done it before; you can do it again.*

I changed clothes, read the instruction booklet, replaced the tire, went back inside, took a shower and dressed for work. *Great,* I thought to myself. *Wait till you tell the women at work and Dr. Grant, as well. Will he be impressed or what?*

But then reality hit when I went back outside, walked up to my car and realized I had changed the wrong tire!

NOW WHAT, O LORD? Am I losing it? I'm laughing and crying at the same time. How silly can I be? You'd think I'd have noticed that the tire I was changing was still inflated. Well, I didn't, so here I am—completely deflated. I know You don't want me to remain in this state, so I pray for Your grace to fill me up and send me on my way—on the bus!

Seedy Salad

Dear God:

Today I was talking with Janet while preparing a simple barbecue lunch. I was excited about this new recipe. In fact, I had taken special care to make a list of the ingredients and even took the list to the supermarket so that I'd be sure to buy everything I needed. I finished tossing the salad, prepared the barbecue ribs and then called to Janet's husband to fire up the grill.

The table was set. And soon the meal was ready. Everyone sat down, and we offered a prayer. We talked and laughed as we passed serving bowls from one to another. Everything looked delicious. I couldn't wait to dig in.

Janet was eager to hear how everyone liked the salad. Suddenly they were all laughing, but my daughter and I didn't have a clue as to why.

It seems the recipe called for sunflower seeds. I had put the seeds in the salad alright, but I'd forgotten to take them out of the shell first! Oh well! What can I say? I'm a senior and I have those moments they talk about. The solution? I told everyone to pick out the seeds and, hopefully, enjoy what was left.

LORD, I DOUBT I'LL EVER LIVE THIS ONE DOWN. Whenever I put out a bowl of salad, everyone starts teasing me about sunflower seeds, and we all laugh. I think I'll focus on my relationship with You instead. All You ask of me is faith the size of a mustard seed. I can handle that.

Dental Visit

Dear God:

I can tell You never intended for us to wear dentures. They simply don't hold up the way our natural teeth do—if we take care of them, that is.

My husband Chuck's lower dentures were once again in two pieces. He had used superglue to repair them many times. One day it was obvious that they simply wouldn't hold up for another round. It was time to see the dentist for a new pair.

Dr. Carter made impressions of both the upper and lower gums for the replacement dentures. As he worked, he asked Chuck, "How long have you had these teeth?"

"Since a car accident in 1960," Chuck responded.

The dentist burst out laughing. "Your dentures are older than I am," he said.

Chuck turned red as he muttered under his breath, "Maybe I should have tried the superglue one more time."

One of the challenges of growing older, Lord, is dealing with the younger crowd. They seem to forget or ignore the fact that they, too, will be seniors one day—complete with false teeth, white hair, hearing aids and books produced in *big print*!

GOD, YOU ARE MY REFUGE in the storms of life and in embarrassing moments—however large or small they may be.

And Justice for All

Dear God:

This is what I get for being in the hurry mode. You cautioned me about it, but sometimes I just don't listen. Today was particularly hectic. I tried to do too much. Before I headed home from the gym and the doctor's office and the cleaners, I ran to the store and picked up some groceries for lunch and dinner.

I put everything away and then started to make lunch. I opened the fridge and reached for the liverwurst. It wasn't there. I looked in the usual place. I was certain I had purchased it. I knew I had been charged for it. Where was it?

I felt my face flush. I was mad—and hungry. I saw only one option: run back to the store to tell the manager my predicament, lodge a complaint and get more liverwurst.

I arrived and went straight to the woman in charge. She was kind enough to check my register receipt, talk to the cashier and then give me another chunk of liverwurst. Satisfied that I had received justice, I dashed home, fixed lunch and served it. My family was happy. Their stomachs were full.

Later that evening as I wiped down the shelves in the refrigerator, I rearranged some food containers. As I opened the vegetable drawer, behold, the original liverwurst appeared.

I returned to the store the next morning—this time with a red face for a different reason than the day before. I was totally embarrassed. I handed the manager enough money to cover the "replacement" she had given me so graciously. She was gracious this time too! As I left the store, I thought I heard the faint sound of laughter in the background.

SOMETIMES IT SEEMS MY HAND IS QUICKER THAN MY MIND. Sometimes? O Lord, much too often these days. But You are there to calm my anxious heart and to encourage me to own up to my mistakes—innocent as some of them are. Who knows? Maybe my willingness to go back to the store was an example of humility that is not often seen in our world today. I hope so.

Lunch on the Run

Dear God:

Hubby and I had been shopping most of the morning and had stopped at a local café for a take-out lunch. We ordered tuna sandwiches and then headed home. We put away the groceries, some into the pantry, some into the refrigerator and others into the garage pantry.

By then we were starved, eager to sit down and enjoy our lunch. However, we couldn't find the sandwiches anywhere. We spent the next 45 minutes retracing our steps. I made a dozen or more trips to the car. I was certain that I had placed the sandwiches on my lap as my husband drove home.

By that time I was sure I had lost both the sandwiches and my mind.

Later that afternoon, I went into the closet where I always hang the car keys along with my purse. There of all places was our lunch, still wrapped up in the take-out package. Apparently, I had placed the bag on the same hook with the keys—without thinking, of course!

LORD, AT THAT POINT I NEED YOU TO TAKE CHARGE OF THE SEARCH. Why didn't I ask You first—before running myself ragged chasing back and forth to the car, when it was clear the food was not there? I'm a slow learner, but You are a patient teacher, and You never lose faith in me. For that I thank You from the bottom of my heart.

Part 4:
Grateful Moments

On the Green

Dear God:

You know what it's like around our house. We could use a few smiles. First Dad, then my brother, Jack, both were diagnosed with cancer 10 days apart. It's hard, Lord, when two of the most important men in my life besides my husband are hit at the same time. We've had to adapt and find something to smile about or we'd all be crying.

The treatments leave them (and me) exhausted and even depressed at times. I'm so grateful You're watching over us through it all.

I sure thank You for the lighthearted moments as well. Last night I phoned Jack and asked how his day had gone. The lilt in his voice surprised me. I couldn't help but smile!

"What have you been up to?" I asked, curious about this burst of energy so late in a day when he had had a treatment.

"I played golf in the morning and then mowed the front and back yards in the afternoon," he boasted.

"I'm impressed," I said, and then tossed him a question for the fun of it.

"Maybe I need a shot of Procrit," I said, referring to his cancer treatment medication. "I need to weed the garden, haul a bag to the recycler, take Mom shopping and do the laundry. I'm tired just thinking about it all."

We both laughed. It's not something we'd normally joke about, but it felt good to share a chuckle.

"I'll ask Dr. F. for you the next time I see him," said Jack. "It might even help you with your golf game!"

We both roared. I've never hit a golf ball in my life and don't have any plans to do so. As for mowing lawns, well, I'll think about it.

WE ARE SO GRATEFUL, LORD, for giving us joy even in this very tough journey. What would we do without You?

$\mathcal{H}$ot Flash

Dear God:

You have blessed my life with so many good things. And now that I'm in the autumn of my life, I'm especially grateful for those small but significant blessings such as the end of the teenage years and curfews. The kids are all grown up now. And thank You for my darling grandchildren who visit and then go home with their parents! I'm relieved to no longer spend money on diapers, school supplies or tuition.

But as I pour out my thanks a question still remains: Why hot flashes? I hear some women never experience this part of aging. It seems like yesterday when I watched my own mother sitting in her chair reading, little brown rivulets running down her neck. (Thank You for brown hair dye today that doesn't run.)

I know You must have a reason—unknown to me—why You have chosen yours truly as the patron saint of menopause! This unnamed plague of the Old Testament can visit me during the day or the night. The outdoor or indoor temperature is irrelevant since my hot flashes hit me in the dead of winter or in the blazing heat of summer. But mostly they occur at the most inopportune times: as I stand in front of a room full of clients preparing to make an important sales presentation, as I sit in a crowded church listening to the sermon or as I am engaged in an animated conversation with a new acquaintance.

Perspiration, as we Southern ladies call it, begins as little droplets around my hairline. Within seconds, the droplets become rivers flowing down my meticulously applied makeup and travel their course through my coiffed hair, turning it into limp, spaghetti-like strands.

Could it be, dear God, wrinkles are really erosion caused by these little rivers? To add to this mortification, the deluge also spreads to the rest of my body. Hot flashes do not spare my new silk blouse or my best Sunday dress. During this soaking, I experience the same heat as a summer day in the middle of the Mojave Desert.

As the attack subsides, leaving a nice glistening effect, I am subject to a rapid cooldown. I quickly bundle myself in the previously discarded jacket or sweater and try to act as though nothing happened.

While some treatments work better than others, none that I have found totally eliminate this curse. Forgive me, please, for my complaints. I should focus on the gift of just being alive!

Though hot flashes do not rank up there with locusts, boils or the trials of Job, it would be so nice to celebrate middle age with a nice sports car like men do rather than a brand new box of black cohosh.

THANK YOU FOR LISTENING, GOD. I feel better already. I remember Your promise to wipe away every tear from my eyes and every pain from my body. Someday I will be made new in heaven with You. Till then, I want to stand fast with my hand in Yours, especially when a hot flash overtakes me!

Éva's Butter Horns

Dear God:

When I think of my mother, I think of her butter horn cookies. Mmm! The kids in our family could polish off a plate of these melt-in-your-mouth cookies in minutes. So when it was my turn to provide dessert for the married couples group my husband and I belong to, I decided to make a batch of butter horns.

I looked in the pantry and fridge for the ingredients and realized I didn't have any of them on hand. Our oven had been on the blitz for months, so I had not been able to bake anything. But the day of the meeting I had no more excuses. We had purchased a new oven when we updated our kitchen.

I drove to the store and purchased flour, butter, cane sugar, powdered sugar, chopped nuts, eggs and salt! Then I remembered I didn't have a rolling pin, so I picked up that too. Total bill: $40.21. Add to that the $1,634.03, the purchase price for the built-in oven, and I could see this was going to be one expensive batch of cookies, let me tell you! (To be exact, each cookie—48 in all—cost $34.88.)

But the worst was yet to come. As I tried to roll out the flour mass (make that mess), the dough stuck to the rolling pin for dear life! I added a bit of flour to the board and to the dough, but no luck. So I started over. Then it dawned on me to flour the rolling pin before rolling out the dough. That helped a bit, but the result was anything but the perfect circle my mother used to make.

It's pretty hard to make rolled-up butter horns (visualize miniature crescent rolls) unless the circle of dough is very thin and very round. After much frustration, I managed to make three-dozen cookies that only vaguely resembled the perfect ones Mom used to make.

However, the guests didn't know the difference. Every cookie vanished from the plate within 10 minutes of my arrival! I was lucky to eat just one, but I was determined to get my $34.88 share.

LORD, THANK YOU FOR MY MOTHER and for the gift of hospitality she modeled. What fun it is to entertain friends and to fix good food and special desserts to share with them. Excuse me, Lord, my mouth is watering for more of those butter horns. I think I'll bake a batch right now.

Recipe for Eva's Butter Horns

Dough:
1 c. butter (softened)
2 c. flour (white or wheat)
1 egg yolk, slightly beaten
¾ c. light sour cream

Filling:
¾ c. sugar
1 t. cinnamon
¾ c. finely chopped nuts (walnuts or pecans)

Directions:
Cut butter into flour. Combine egg yolk and sour cream. Blend with flour mixture. Form into ball and cover with waxed paper. Chill in refrigerator overnight or for several hours before baking.

Divide dough into three parts. Roll each part into a circle about 12″ in diameter. Cut each circle into 16 wedges with knife or pizza cutter.

Prepare the filling. Combine sugar, cinnamon and nuts. Sprinkle mixture over the dough. Roll each wedge, starting with the wide end, shaping it into crescents.

Bake on ungreased cookie sheet at 375 degrees Fahrenheit for about 20 minutes until light brown. Remove from cookie sheet to cool. Dust with powdered sugar.

Share and enjoy!

$\mathcal{K}$ey Point

Dear God:

It must have been the heat! It was over 100 degrees in Riverside, according to the weather report. I certainly felt it—especially when I got out of my car at the strip mall and went into the nail salon to make an appointment. Generally, when I get out of my car, as You know, I hook my keys to the ring attached to my purse or I clip it to the lanyard around my neck. I'm pleased to say I've never misplaced my car keys in 50 years of driving.

You can imagine my concern then when I got into my car and couldn't find the keys anywhere. I panicked. I checked the usual places. It was not around my neck. It was not attached to my purse. Did I drop it in the shop? I wondered as my heart pounded. I was about to get out of the car and retrace my steps when I calmed down enough to hear a faint humming.

It was coming from the engine of my car. The car was in gear. It was turned on, so where was my key? Why in the ignition where it belonged.

I tossed up a quick prayer of thanks and pulled out of the driveway, chagrined, but grateful and relieved.

GOD, I AM AMAZED at the level of confusion and panic I can succumb to when I forget to go to You first. Every time I rely on my own understanding I blow it. Maybe that's why You remind us in Scripture to lean on You and not on our own understanding (see Prov. 3:5). May I remember that next time. And if I don't, please tap me on the shoulder!

North Pole or South?

Dear God:

My new tent is supposed to be a breeze to open. You saw the advertisement: "Two-minute setup. Even a child can put up this tent." But it didn't say anything about people in their second childhood!

I got to the campground and watched in awe as the other campers swished and whisked and staked and raked. Next thing I knew I was surrounded by a colorful array of large and small tents, but mine was still in the bag.

I pulled it out, flipped it this way and that, and finally it opened. Before it collapsed on the spot, I grabbed the stakes, pounded them into the ground and secured the tent. (It took a lot longer than two minutes, by the way!)

Someone suggested I add the rain fly just in case the weather turned. I threw it over the top of the tent and staked it as best I could. I didn't see how it would do much good, though, since it clung so closely to the tent itself. Oh well.

Later in the week, someone asked why I hadn't used the rear tent pole. No wonder the rain fly looked so limp. There was nothing to hold it up.

I looked among my gear, but it wasn't there. Then I remembered. When I opened the tent at home, I had set the poles to one side as I read the instructions. Apparently, I repacked the sack but left one pole out by mistake.

Lord, it's tough being a senior. Just when you think you have all your tent pegs and poles in a row, you find out you left one at home—and it's often the very one you need most!

IS IT ANY WONDER, LORD, THAT I NEED AS MUCH HELP AS I DO? I'm simply unfit to keep it altogether without Your wisdom and direction. It doesn't mean I'm a fool or a misfit, just a human being who is blessed to have You, my God, to depend on—when I can't seem to do life on my terms.

Alarming News

Dear God:

I am fed up with these car alarms that go off in the middle of a parking lot, in the middle of our condo's parking garage, in the middle of a good night's sleep.

But I am even more frustrated when I hear one in a campground—the very place I come to get away from such city noises. You can imagine my irritation last week when I was settling down for a much-needed rest and I suddenly heard, ra-ra-ra, boing-boing-boing, whir-whir-whir.

It seemed whichever way I turned I couldn't tune it out. I was about to stomp out of my tent and shout across the campground, "Whose car is ranting and raving? Do something and do it now! We're trying to get some sleep around here." But I didn't. I was too scared and too cold.

Finally, I turned on my back and lay still. I prayed the sound would die down and eventually stop. It did—or maybe I just fell asleep and didn't hear it any longer.

After my trip was over, I drove home and didn't think any more about sirens and bells! I was just glad to be in my own house. But can You believe it, God? The very first night I was home, I heard a car siren go off right in front of my house. I was dozing on the living room sofa when suddenly that familiar sound blared. *Here we go again*, I thought. *I can't seem to get away from it.*

I reached into my pocket for my house key, so I could go out front and check to see if I recognized the car. Then I could go to the right neighbor and let him or her know.

As I moved my hand, the siren stopped. I pulled out my set of keys and then it suddenly hit me. I remembered the car salesman telling me that the safety system is highly sensitive. If you press the combination lock key carelessly it will discharge the alarm.

I felt my face flush. How embarrassing. I was the culprit here at home *and* the one in the campground. I had kept my keys in my pocket at night in my sleeping bag so I wouldn't lose them. Apparently, every time I turned, I pressed on the lock and it set off the alarm.

There I was blaming someone else for my own senior moment.

LORD, HOW QUICKLY I SHIFT THE RESPONSIBILITY TO SOMEONE ELSE before I have all the facts. No wonder You remind us in Scripture that You will instruct us and teach us in the way we should go (see Ps. 32:8). And in the way we should turn when we have keys in our pockets!

Matching Caps

Dear God:

Here's a good laugh—and a good example of a bona fide senior moment. My friend's grandson hiked to the top of Mount Whitney, the highest peak in the continental United States, which stands at more than 14,000 feet. He was so proud of this accomplishment.

When he came back from the trip, he rushed over to his grandmother's house to tell her the news and to boast of his accomplishment by donning a cap that read: "I Made It to the Top of Mount Whitney."

She congratulated him and told him how proud of him she was. As he was leaving, he noticed one of her sun hats on a table by the front door. It looked a lot like his. He picked it up and read the wording stitched across the front: "I Hiked Mount Whitney."

"Grandma," he said, impressed with what he read, "I didn't know you climbed Mount Whitney too. Why didn't you tell me?"

Grandma looked bewildered for a moment. Then she read the words herself. It was the first time she had really seen what they said. "Oh no, I didn't hike Mount Whitney," she said, a bit embarrassed. "I just bought a hat one day while passing through Lone Pine, California, because I had forgotten mine at home."

Back to basics: Reading 101.

HERE'S A GOOD LESSON FOR ME. I need to open my eyes to what's going on around me or I might be giving out the wrong information or taking credit when it's not due me! Thank You, God, for looking out for my every going out and coming in.

Dedication

Dear God:

Remember the book I wrote for teens 20 years ago about careers in the zoo? What a project that was. I spent many hours interviewing zoo personnel, checking facts, and typing and retyping the manuscript before delivering it to the publisher.

My husband, Charles, was very supportive, so I dedicated the book to him. Little did we know at the time that it would become a great prop when he became a tour guide in our town.

One of his favorite assignments is taking a busload of people to San Diego's world-famous zoo and Wild Animal Park. Part of his job is to keep the clients happy with a bit of humor and history as they drive from one location to the next.

As the bus driver pulls into the zoo parking lot, Charles now takes out a copy of my book, holds it up for all to see and suggests they purchase their very own copy. Then he says with a wry smile, "Folks, what do you think of this? My wife writes children's books among other things, and here's one that applies to the topic of today's trip. The title is *Maybe You Belong in the Zoo*. Then he pauses thoughtfully and announces, "The only problem is she dedicated the book to me! How's that for a senior moment? It does not seem smart to me to dedicate such a title to the man you sleep with every night!"

The tourists howl, Charles is happy, and I sell a few more books!

GOD, THANK YOU FOR providing us with fun and finances. It is such a good feeling to share my writing talent with others, to entertain and inform them, and to remind them through my writing of Your many gifts to each one of us—if we but look for them.

Little Red Wagon

Dear God:

I remember my father buying me a little red wagon for my fifth birthday. I used it for hauling toys, giving Pepper a ride when she was too tired to walk and taking turns pulling friends around the yard.

I gave it away when I got older. I was 10 when I passed it on to a younger cousin. I never would have thought that 60 years later I'd be wishing I kept it. But that's a fact. I told my friend Nell about the wagon, and we had a good laugh. Then for my birthday this week, she gave me a little red wagon. I about cried when she led me out to the yard to see it. I felt like five years old all over again. Nell had loaded it with new gardening tools and supplies. She knows how much I like to work in my vegetable garden and flower beds.

"Now you'll have everything in one place," she said. "You won't have to put up with any more of those senior moments you've been telling me about. Everything's in one place, and there's a place for each thing." She stepped back and admired her gift.

I had fun unwrapping each item and thinking about much I would enjoy using the brand new fork and shiny trowel, and planting the flower seeds. She also had slipped in a new pair of gardening gloves and a matching apron and cap. I was sure I'd be the talk of the neighborhood with all this gear.

THANK YOU, LORD, for thoughtful friends who see a need and fill it. You're the most faithful friend of all. You saw my real need before I was born, and You sent Jesus to fill it. I thank You, too, that I can still garden at my age.

Black and Blue

Dear God:

My students caught me today. And I was the only one to defend myself! I guess I really am a senior, after all, much as I resist it. While getting ready for school this morning, I was preoccupied, as usual, with so many thoughts: lesson plans, parent-teacher conferences and my grocery list! In addition, it was a cloudy day, dark and dreary with the threat of rain. I felt out of sorts and didn't pay much attention to what I pulled out of the closet. I slipped into my comfy shoes, knowing I'd be on my feet more than usual this day.

After I arrived at my classroom, a couple of students popped in early and asked if they could help. Just as I said, "Sure," the two broke into laughter as they pointed at my feet.

"What's so funny?" I asked, feeling a bit indignant.

Then I, too, let out a howl as I realized that I was wearing a navy shoe on my right foot and a black shoe on my left foot. Anyone passing my room probably thought I was having a wild party from the sound of our laughter.

At first, I was too embarrassed to share it with anyone else, but then decided at lunch that we all could use a light moment on this dark day. All the teachers enjoyed my tale of how I had gotten black and blue!

THANK YOU, LORD, that from Your point of view, my relationship with You does not depend on style or color. You care about the condition of my heart and the attitude of my mind.

Musical Beds

Dear God:

It has been a blessing to have my mother-in-law with us while recuperating from hip surgery. I didn't want her to climb the stairs to the guest room, so we played musical beds. She slept in our bed, my son moved to the guest room and Mike and I slept in our son's room.

As You know, children don't like to take their parents' advice, and it seems parents don't relish listening to their grown children. I'm no exception. My son distinctly told me to leave his alarm clock alone and it would ring at 6:00 A.M. Did I listen? No! I looked at the clock and saw a button that said, "Alarm Off/Reset." I pushed it down and nothing seemed to happen, so I didn't think about it again. I was simply curious! No harm done.

That is until Mike and I went to sleep. Suddenly, in the dead of the night, the alarm went off. My husband shut it off as usual. I got up and went downstairs for breakfast. As I was about to cut my banana over a bowl of cereal, I glanced at the clock: 2:45 A.M. Hmmm! A bit early for breakfast.

I put the cereal away and wrapped up the banana. Then I padded back to bed and told Mike what had happened. He was glad he had rolled over for another five minutes! He wondered why he felt so exhausted. We had a good laugh and then fell back to sleep. That morning I reset my son's clock—and never said a thing about it!

LORD, I DO THE DARNEDEST things sometimes. I often wonder how I ever got along before I knew You as my friend. You
were there, weren't You, even when I didn't realize it? Thank You.

All in Vain!

Dear God:

I've noticed that many (but not all) women go to extreme measures to hide the fact that they've undergone cosmetic or "vanity" surgery.

Who are they trying to kid? The cleavage reveals their secret. The cup used to be half-empty, but now it "runneth over"—even at 60 or 70.

"Miraculous results," the advertising states.

It surely would be a miracle at my age.

Remember years ago when Iris had her eyes "done"? She begged our friend Rita to keep her secret, not to breathe a word to anyone. But Rita did breathe it to me—in more than one word. When I saw Iris, even without a heads-up, I would have noticed her newly tightened eyelids and the obvious absence of crow's-feet. Iris's Irish eyes were smiling alright, and she did look younger.

But not all plastic surgeries go smoothly. I remember several years ago, a woman I call Polly was turning 50. She decided, with the encouragement of her family, that she needed a face-lift.

Polly, too, wanted the surgery to be a secret. I don't know what she planned to say when people looked at her after the procedure. She had a striking resemblance to her 20-something daughter. Oops, her hands gave her away! But that's not all.

Her friend, Diane, was instructed to be tight-lipped about Polly's soon-to-be tight lips, eyes, cheeks and jaw. Polly's face would be tight alright—achingly tight, skin-ripping tight. The surgeon got a little carried away with the scalpel and thought he could turn back the clock on Polly's face to the Roaring Twenties. Polly roared alright—and not from the delight of looking twentysomething. The surgeon had stretched the skin on her cheeks so tight that it actually pulled apart within a few days after the surgery.

In pain and emotional distress, Polly went back to the surgeon several times to repair the damage. For months, she wore heavy makeup to cover the scarring.

But the best part is that Polly's face-lift fiasco led to a "faith-lift." She learned through painful personal experience the truth of Jesus' words: "There is nothing concealed that will not be disclosed, or hidden that will not be made known" (Luke 12:2).

I MAY NEVER LIFT MY FACE, but, Lord, I want to lift my eyes, my hands and my voice to You in prayerful thanksgiving—for You and You alone are the lifter of my head.

Part 5: Tug-at-the-Heart Moments

Teacup Pup

Dear God:

Thank You for my darling little teacup-sized Chihuahua. She is such a comfort to me. This morning, though, I was anything but a comfort to her. I was so busy getting ready to leave the house to catch an early morning flight—4:30 A.M. to be exact—I let Missy out by herself for her morning ritual. Normally, I watch her very carefully, because she is as small as a rabbit and would make a tasty morsel for an owl, hawk or coyote.

But today I was so focused on myself that I forgot all about her. Not only did I forget to let her back in, I forgot that I let her out! What's happening to me?

John got up an hour later and heard a tiny whining sound coming from outside. He opened the door and, sure enough, there was little Missy shivering in the cold. I shudder just thinking about this experience and what could have happened to her.

THANK YOU FOR LOOKING OUT FOR LITTLE MISSY and for me, O God. This is just a glimpse of Your thoughtful care and protection over all Your creatures, myself included.

Missing Parts

Dear God:

Today Dad and I went to visit Aunt Ethel. I was sorry to see her in such declining health. I guess I see myself in her—20 years in the future. It's scary to think about. But I do enjoy her sense of humor. Maybe I inherited that too. I hope so, because I'm going to need it. Come to think of it, I need it right now!

I remember sitting in Auntie's living room as she and Dad commiserated over their conditions. She was nearly blind from diabetes and almost deaf to the point of having to give up independent living.

I had to chuckle when she leaned over and in a loud voice told Dad, "It doesn't bother me too much about not hearing as well as I used to. We have to expect our sight to change as we get older." Then with a twinkle in her pale blue eyes, she quipped, "But I sure do miss my mind!"

Lord God, glimpses into my future through the experiences of others have been a big help in my aging. I am less fearful knowing You are with me and more conscious of the precious time I have right now.

HELP ME TO BE MINDFUL of each second of each day and to make the most of the things I can see, hear, smell, touch and taste.

$\mathcal{P}$ushy Fellow

Dear God:

Remember the gentleman at the nursing home known as the "push-me-back" man? No matter who was standing around, even if he didn't know the person, he'd maneuver his wheelchair up to that person and say, "Push me back."

No one knew where he wanted to be pushed back to! Other than that one phrase, he never spoke. He just wheeled himself around the facility. I'm thinking of that one day when I arrived just in time to feed Daddy his dinner.

Across the room, push-me-back's wife was feeding him. The room was typically silent, since most of the people could not speak, and those who could were busy eating.

Suddenly, push-me-back swallowed the next forkful of food, looked up at his wife and, as clear as a bell, spoke aloud for all to hear: "I wonder if the tax laws have changed much this year."

WHAT A BLESSING, LORD, THAT BY THE END OF LIFE, most of us can relax and simply observe the passing scene—and comment on it when we want to! We are assured of our place in Your presence when the time is right to join You in heaven.

Misplaced Place Mat

Dear God:

How funny and strange! Yesterday while dumping some trash into the compactor, I caught sight of a bit of lace. Before I turned on the compactor, I pulled out the delicate piece. I discovered a neatly folded cloth and lace-trimmed place mat—the last of a set of six. I had wondered where it had disappeared. I thought maybe it was trapped behind the washing machine or dryer. I remember telling myself, "I'll get to it one day, when someone's here to help me."

This turned out to be *the* day—and *You* are with me. We didn't even have to move heavy appliances to look for it. You brought it to my attention when I least expected it.

I sat down for a moment and thought about this sweet surprise among the trash. Isn't this so like You to help me see the light in the darkness, the joy instead of the hurt, the highs instead of the lows?

I like this stage of my life, when I can stop and contemplate, instead of panicking over every mistake I make. I hear You speak to me in such moments, with compassion and tenderness, reminding me that, above all, I am Yours. You will never toss me on a heap of trash! To You, I'm a treasure worth dying for.

LORD, IF IT WEREN'T FOR YOU, what would become of me as I age? But I can stop worrying. In fact, You command Your children not to worry (see Matt. 6:25,28,31,34). You will supply all of my needs, even if I misplace or lose something. All I really need comes from Your generous hand—whether an extra measure of grace or a lovely lace-trimmed place mat.

Junk Mail

Dear God:

What can I do about all the junk mail I receive every day? I'm drowning in this stuff, but I hate to throw anything away. What if I need it someday? That offer for new dentures or a way to pay my bills without writing checks? Maybe I'll be glad I hung on to it.

My daughter-in-law likes to come in and shred the stuff, but I'm not sure it's a good idea. I remember my mother saving rubber bands and cardboard backs from Dad's starched shirts. I guess that's what happens to those of us raised during the Depression. "It might come in handy some day," Mom used to crow when I wanted to dump a load of paper into the trash. Now here I am behaving just like she did.

Maybe I can find a happy medium: save the mail for a week, and if I can't find any use for it by then, send it to the shredder. Now there's a concept—a clutter-free apartment. Then I'd have space around me for the things I love: books and old records and good friends to laugh and talk with.

Hey, I'm feeling energized again. Now where's that pile of mail? This is as good a time as any to get rid of it. And what about those old shoes and the bathrobe I've had for 20 years, and the magazines in the closet and those skirts and blouses and sweaters and jackets in boxes in the garage?

Out with the old and in with the new me, ready for whatever comes next. Lead me on, Lord.

I LOVE IT, LORD, when You give me these good ideas—the ones I'm too frugal or fearful to put into action on my own. You also give me the strength to carry them out.

Disappearing Act

Dear God:

Aren't You just a bit fed up with Your people misplacing things, forgetting stuff and losing items day after day after day? Will we ever learn? I'm not betting on it.

On Sunday morning, just as my husband and I were leaving for church, he discovered that he had misplaced his sunglasses. He walked around the house mumbling and grumbling and tossing things here and there during his search.

"I need your help," he confessed. "I'm absolutely positive I put them on the dining room table, and now they've totally disappeared."

Instead of being the gracious and helpful wife—the one You talk about in Proverbs 31—I lectured him about misplacing things. He was not a happy camper, especially this day, because he is never late for church—ever.

This exchange led to a spat. I was ready to leave without him, when he looked at me with a quizzical expression on his face. "Are those your glasses you're wearing?" he asked.

I took them off and, sure enough, I was wearing his. We both have the same brand and they look alike. I checked my purse. Mine were in the case where I had last put them. Sheepishly, I admitted I was wearing his pair of sunglasses.

We arrived at church on time, though we didn't say one word to each other in the car. I don't like it when senior moments go too far. I owe my husband an apology, and I need to confess my prideful stance to You, dear God.

THANK YOU FOR SHOWING US THE TRUTH and for giving us the freedom to cool down before reminding us that we are one flesh and we need to treat one another with love and tenderness, respect and forgiveness. I'm going to make this right between us right now.

$\mathcal{F}$inal Journey

Dear God:

It's hard to watch Mom on the final leg of her journey home. I thank You for her long life. Eighty-six! But I'm concerned about her after the massive heart attack and stroke. I'm amazed she can keep on as well as she has.

The part that's really hard is knowing she's losing her ability to speak to us. Mom was always so good with words. I miss our conversations. With Dad being profoundly deaf and Mom unable to speak, we make an interesting threesome. We are being challenged to find new ways to communicate with each other. And I am having an opportunity to serve Mom in a way I never would have imagined or chosen.

I'm sad when I think of what is likely ahead for us. But I'm also grateful to be reminded through all this that You are in control and have a plan for us, separately and collectively. Thank You for my parents, God.

May I focus on the good, release the not so good and trust You with the eternal results.

I PRAISE YOU, LORD, for showing me new and unselfish ways to relate to my mother and father, to express my love, and to help them during this frightening and often uncertain time in their lives. It is also good for me to see that as a senior myself, I am changing physically, mentally and emotionally. And more than ever I want to depend on You.

Lockdown

Dear God:

It helps to read the manual, I know, now that I've made a series of pretty silly mistakes with my new pickup truck.

After shopping in the mall, I walked out to the parking lot and clicked my remote key. I wanted the truck to be unlocked and ready for me to jump into without hesitation. I promised my husband, Ron, that I'd be vigilant about my safety, especially when I'm alone in a parking lot after dark.

But when I arrived at the truck and grabbed the door handle, it wouldn't budge. I tugged and tugged again. No change. I panicked. What was wrong? I hit the remote button a second time and this time the door opened without a hitch.

Then it hit me. The door is setup to relock after a few seconds if the driver does not open it. It's a good safety feature—if one knows about it. Now I know because I read the manual after I returned home.

THIS EXPERIENCE REMINDED ME that I need to brush up on the instructions in Your manual. The Bible provides so much wisdom for everyday life. When I tug at the door of a situation that won't budge, I panic too quickly. If I would turn to Your Word each day, I'd know just what to do, and no event or person would be too much for me to handle.

$\mathcal{C}$ircumstantial Evidence

Dear God:

What did You think of me this morning? What could be more embarrassing? I thought I was completely ready to call the congregation to prayer for our nation and for our president. I had spent some time putting together just the right wording. I ran it by my wife. I practiced it out loud. I went over it silently in bed before getting up. And then I arrived at church and this momentous occasion suddenly turned humorous.

I wanted to thank You, Lord, for Your many blessings in all circumstances. But as You know, the words did not come out the way I planned. "Let us thank God for being with us in all circumcisions!" I said.

My face flushed and the congregation burst into laughter. I couldn't contain myself for long. I laughed too, even though I felt like fleeing the scene. I ended with a resounding "Amen." Needless to say, I did not welcome standing in the back of the church as people filed past me with a grin and said, "Hey, Pastor Jim, nice prayer this morning!"

That's what I get, Lord, for trying to do two things at once: preparing for my teaching on Jewish law, which included circumcision, and getting ready for my sermon on God's faithfulness in all circumstances!

GOD, I FEEL BLESSED at a time like this to know You are smiling with me and reminding me that no error is too big for You to forgive and forget, and for letting me know that humor is often the very thing needed to draw people to You. May I never get too serious for my own good!

$\mathscr{S}$pare Me!

Dear God:

Please slow me down. I'm becoming a danger to myself. My to-do list this morning was a page long. I put off so many of the things I don't like to be bothered with, but I could no longer hide from them. I tucked the list in my purse, grabbed the car keys and headed out to the garage.

I felt a strong breeze and decided it was wise to take a jacket, just in case a storm developed. So I trotted back inside, set my purse and keys on the kitchen counter, and grabbed a jacket from the hall closet.

I slammed the door hard as I left, assuring myself that it was locked tight. It certainly was when I tried to open it, after I realized I had left my purse and keys inside the house. Bummer!

Thankfully, we keep spare keys in the garage, so I calmed down when I realized that was the case. I opened the box where we store them, but it was empty. My heart started pounding again.

I'll call Bill at work, I told myself. *He won't like having to drive back home so soon after arriving at the office, but what else can I do?*

I reached for my cell phone and then realized it, too, was in the purse in the house. Rats! I felt stuck. Wait! I could go to my neighbor's house and use her phone. What a blessing! She was home and she was happy to let me make the phone call.

Bill's voice mail said he was out for the day on sales calls and would not be taking cell phone messages, either, because he had left his phone at home by mistake. He promised to return calls at the end of the day.

Great! I thought. *I'm so close yet so far from home.* I decided to be creative—after I had a good cry over my thoughtlessness. I chose to make this a good thing. I took my bike out of the garage and biked along the lake near our home. I knew I could visit a neighbor. There were plenty of people who would have taken me in, but I used the time instead to be alone and quiet.

As for the missing spare keys? Bill took them that morning when he, too, walked out without his keys. He didn't want to ring the bell, because he knew I was in the shower. There You have it, Lord, a senior moment turned into a joyful moment that led to gratitude about how You always bring everything together for good to those who love You (see Rom. 8:28).

AND LORD, HOW I DO LOVE YOU, and I know that You love me.

$\mathscr{S}$imple Gifts

Dear God:

I love the old Shaker tune, "'tis a gift to be simple, 'tis a gift to be free, 'tis a gift to come down where you ought to be." It means even more to me now that I'm a senior. Being free and humble is just where I ought to be—every day!

I recall a day long ago when I received the gentle message this song has to offer. Remember, Lord, how Charles and I had worked hard all day in the yard of our little mountain hideaway pruning tree limbs, cutting back flower beds and pulling persistent weeds? By four o'clock all I wanted was a warm tub and a bowl of hot soup!

At that moment, I wasn't so sure we had made the right decision to buy an old fixer-upper over 100 miles away from our permanent home. We had thought it would be "fun" when we signed the escrow papers and wrote the check for the down payment, but now it felt like nothing but work!

And I was living proof of the labor it required. I glanced in the mirror in the bathroom and was ashamed to see what a mess I was: broken fingernails, matted-down hair, a red face from too much sun, droopy eyes, and scratches up and down my arms and legs.

Charles stayed behind to put away the gardening tools. I was relieved he didn't have to see me up close. At last, I settled into the soapy water, took a deep breath and relaxed for the first time that day. But not for long.

My thoughts raced ahead of me. I was determined to turn this place into something that was worth the effort and the money we had invested. I gave my imagination complete freedom as I renovated and decorated every square inch of the place in my mind.

A hard rap on the bathroom window pulled me out of my fantasy. I ran my hand over the steamy windowpane and looked out. There stood Charles smiling at me, his face smudged, his eyes bright. He pulled off his cap and wiped the beads of perspiration that trickled down his face.

"What's up?" I called.

"Not much," he answered. "I miss you, that's all. The sun's almost down," he added gently, pointing toward the mountains, "and I want you here beside me as the day ends."

A little shiver ran down my spine. Here was a gesture so simple, a gift so lovely, it took my breath away—and brought me down to where I ought to be. I suddenly had a fresh vision of You, dear Jesus, in my husband's words and in his face. What did it matter, in that moment, that we didn't have everything in place? We had You. We had each other. We had this day. Tomorrow would take care of itself.

I suddenly became aware of what a gift it is to be simple—and to be free.

I grabbed a towel, slipped into my bathrobe and dashed out back, just in time to enjoy the simple pleasure of watching, arm-in-arm with my husband, the golden sun slip behind the hills.

THANK YOU, GOD, for the gift of sunrises and sunsets, for my mate's loving arms, for flowers and trees, and for shrubs, even if they do need to be trimmed and pruned. You are here with me in the work and in the rewards. What more could I want?

Apple Slices

Dear God:

It was agonizing to watch Mom decline and then to receive word that she had died in her sleep. But that alone was an answer to prayer. I had asked You for months to please take her peacefully as she lay sleeping.

It was difficult to imagine her time here on Earth coming to an end. I kept thinking of her as the young, vibrant mother I remember from my youth. She was my Girl Scouts leader, schoolroom mom and seamstress extraordinaire. And she could bake apple slices to die for! My mouth waters just thinking about them.

But I will never taste them again—at least not from *her* hand. I miss her and the times we shared—whether over the stove, over a good book, over a cup of tea or over a good conversation. She's with You now. Lucky You, Lord! (I hope You don't mind my saying so!) I know You are taking good care of her.

She was a senior with flair, with pizzazz, with dazzle, with *class*.

I hope I'm like her at least a little bit as I grow older and as I, like her, notice more and more of those senior moments that we both used to laugh about.

LORD, I'M GRATEFUL for my mother. She was not only beautiful on the outside but a beauty within too. And I know she loves You as You love her.

New Friend

Dear God:

What a nice surprise You arranged today, when I was feeling alone, scared and out of my element. I didn't want to move in with my daughter, but it seemed to be *that* time. I needed help, and she wanted to give it to me.

I looked around my beautiful new room, decorated with my own furnishings and even my favorite wall paintings. Then I sat down and cried!

What happened? I wondered. *Where did all the years go? Here I am in my late seventies when it seemed only yesterday that I was a girl of 20, engaged to Fred and excited about the two of us setting up our own home together.*

I wondered if I'd ever feel at home in this big house, on this block where I didn't know another soul. It was fine to visit my daughter, but *live* with her? I wasn't so sure in that moment.

Then suddenly there was a knock at the door. I answered it and there stood a woman with a friendly face and gray hair and wrinkles just like mine! She had come to welcome me to the neighborhood.

Then she handed me a lovely tin filled with candy and cookies she had made herself. Tears welled in my eyes—this time from gratitude, not grief. I had a new friend, and so did she. We took an instant liking to one another.

Meg is her name. We're going for a walk tomorrow morning, and she's going to introduce me to her quilting group. She even suggested that I consider joining them. How did she know that I've had a half-finished quilt for about five years now?

SWEET LORD, YOU DO THINK OF EVERYTHING, don't You? You mean it when You say that You will take care of us in every way all the days of our lives (see Ps. 23:6).

Peak Experience

Dear God:

When I turned 50, I vowed I'd do something outrageous, outstanding, even outlandish! Well, I did, and You helped me succeed.

I had wanted to hike in the mountains ever since I was a kid when I saw my first real mountain in Phoenix, Arizona. Forty-some years later, I got the chance. A trip to Half Dome in Yosemite National Park came to my attention through the Sierra Club. I signed up right away—before I got scared and changed my mind. I spent months getting in shape with weekly workouts and learned all I could about tents and boots and backpacks and dehydrated food.

Then came the day for the climb up the steep rock face. I took a deep breath and looked out! Remember how my heart pounded? I wanted to capture this moment forever. In front of me and to the sides—up, down and everywhere I gazed—was a banquet of massive pines, giant cliffs, powerful boulders and high peaks positioned against a deep blue sky. I could scarcely take it in. What a moment for this senior who had been aching for years to experience this opportunity in person.

I remember thinking to myself, *This is a holy place. God is here.* And You were—and are! You thought of everything. Thank You for cool water from a rushing stream to quench my thirst, for fire under my miniature stove to heat my food and warm my feet, and for the cluster of boulders and rocks and a few sturdy tree limbs—the only furniture required. A bed of pine needles made a comfortable carpet for my tent. A broad old tree provided stumps for seats, limbs for hanging wet socks and branches for shade.

You were with me in that wild place in a way I had never known before. How could I not notice Your presence? Why even the stones cried out!

O LORD, YOU ARE SO GOOD TO ME. It took me half a century to reach my goal, but I reached it—and You were with me all the way, just as You are during all the ups and downs of my life. With you leading and guiding me, every day is a peak experience.

$\mathcal{B}$arbecue

Dear God:

I loved hearing stories about Pastor Harry and his amazing faith. Why the day he died, he sat up in bed comforting those who came to say good-bye. He was the cheerleader. "Don't be sorry for me," he told his friends and neighbors. "I'm going to see Jesus any moment now. Feel sorry for yourselves, cause your turn hasn't come up yet!" Then he'd laugh and tell another one of his corny jokes. Folks around him laughed and cried at the same time as they filed in and out of his little Arkansas home.

Harry had been their friend, pastor, counselor, neighbor, prayer warrior and more. They all loved him and were so sad to seem him go. Especially those who had received his famous barbecue chickens. He was known for his little missions, delivering hot food to the needy, even to strangers. He prayed for guidance, and when God told him to do something, he did it—without a whimper.

One day he heard the word "chicken" during his morning prayer time, so he ordered a batch of barbecued chickens and drove the neighborhood, dropping off a bird or two at whichever door You led him to. It turned out that every one of those people were in need that day. One was too ill to go to the store. Another was homebound with two sick children. Others were simply too old to cook for themselves.

Every person was blessed. It was as though Harry had the gift of multiplication, but instead of loaves and fishes, it was barbecue chickens. He bought up a bunch and, in the end, he had *exactly* enough to feed everyone on Your list.

What a way to spend your senior moments—and years—serving You, Lord, by serving others.

WE WILL NOT SOON FORGET those who have blessed us with their gifts, for we know they come from You. Thank You for loving us in our time of need and in all times.

Homemade Memories

Dear God:

Today I'm thinking about the beautiful quilt my mother-in-law made me when I was a young bride. She handed it to me and said tenderly, "I made it for you, but I hope you'll pass it on to one of your children one day. I'd like to think of it as a love link from one generation to the next."

At the time, I couldn't imagine getting to that point in my life, but here I am, a senior just like Momma Rose was when she gave me the quilt. When I die, it will go to my daughter and then to my granddaughter. Lord, Your Word is like that quilt. It covers me but never smothers me. And it is a *living* Word that I can pass on to future generations so they too will know of Your love for them and Your eternal plan for their lives.

You tell us, Lord, to pass on Your teachings to those who come after us. If we train up a child in Your ways, he or she will always return to them. I believe that to be true. It happened in my life.

Today, the quilt, our first Bible and other treasured heirlooms (baby shoes, handmade doilies, a Shirley Temple cereal bowl, my first dictionary) are on display in a glass-front bookcase in the front hall of our home. This collection of treasures serves as an anchor to the past and a bridge to the future, where You have prepared a place for each of us.

I LOOK FORWARD to that day, O Lord, when I will be with You forever in person, rejoicing with the saints over the promises You have fulfilled.

A Note from the Editors

This book was selected by the Books and Inspirational Media Division of Guideposts, the world's leading inspirational publisher. Founded in 1945 by Dr. Norman Vincent Peale and his wife Ruth Stafford Peale, Guideposts helps people from all walks of life achieve their maximum personal and spiritual potential. Guideposts is committed to communicating positive, faith-filled principles for people everywhere to use in successful daily living.

Our publications include award-winning magazines such as *Guideposts*, *Angels on Earth* and *Positive Thinking*, best-selling books, and outreach services that demonstrate what can happen when faith and positive thinking are applied in day-to-day life.

For more information, visit us online at www.guideposts.com, call (800) 431-2344 or write Guideposts, PO Box 5815, Harlan, Iowa 51593.